SPEECH
COMMUNICATION

Concepts and Behavior

SPEECH COMMUNICATION

Concepts and Behavior

FRANK E. X. DANCE

Professor of Speech Communication
University of Denver

CARL E. LARSON

Associate Professor of Speech Communication
University of Denver

HOLT, RINEHART AND WINSTON, INC.

New York	*Chicago*	*San Francisco*
Atlanta	*Dallas*	*Montreal*
Toronto	*London*	*Sydney*

Copyright © 1972 by Holt, Rinehart and Winston, Inc.
All rights reserved.

Library of Congress Catalog Card Number: 75-187117

0-03-080088-9

PRINTED IN THE UNITED STATES OF AMERICA

2 3 4 5 6   038   9 8 7 6 5 4 3 2 1

With so many basic speech texts on the market, why would anyone write or publish an additional one? We believe that this is a legitimate question that calls for an answer. We prepared this book for the following reasons:

1. A basic text should include both theory and practice; there is no legitimate conflict between the two. This book includes theory based on current research and speculation as well as practice designed to indicate some experiential applications and values of the theory.

Although we share a belief in and a commitment to the value of practice, we are aware that our efforts to pair theoretical points with practical applications sometimes fall short of our desires. The successful synthesis of theory and practice is most often the result of student effort under the guidance of an informed, compassionate facilitator/teacher. We recognize and appreciate that much of the success of our efforts in this book depends on the work of our colleagues in the classroom—both faculty and students.

2. New research warrants new publications. Within the past decade new material of primary interest to speech communication scholars has been developed by experimentalists and empiricists in America, the Soviet Union, and elsewhere. New rhetorical insights are being offered by phenomenological philosophers; new clinical applications by social psychologists and analytical psychiatrists; new cross-cultural insights by cognitive anthropologists and political scientists; new ways of viewing the mechanisms involved by neurologists, pathologists, audiologists; and new esthetic and ethical judgments come from many sources. Although we cannot promise to have touched on, much less treated fully, all such material, we have tried to make the materials presented represent the best current interdisciplinary research and thought concerning speech communication.

3. A basic speech text should cover performance, because in speech communication performance *is* content. Skill is not a frill, but

an essential part of communication. The respect of both of us for the role of performance informs our writing.

4. The spoken word is central to speech communication. This is not a textbook in general communication theory or rhetorical composition. It *is* a textbook in speech communication, the study of spoken symbolic interaction.

5. Our field is essential to human knowledge and self-actualization. Speech communication is an academic necessity at all levels of education. This book views speech communication as having intellectual and experiential applications warranting serious study. The book is meant to be a first book, but *not* a primer. It is designed to present the discipline in a way that will excite the high-quality student and yet will be practical enough to satisfy all students' demands for academic relevance.

6. The time has come for efforts to be made in the direction of general theory construction in speech communication. This book represents one such effort. Lee Thayer once wrote,

> ... disciplines are developed in reverse order of their significance to the human existence. If that be true, a comprehensive and heuristic theory of human communication will surely be the last theory to be developed by the scientific community.[1]

We do not conceive of our efforts in theory construction as either total or final—they are simply efforts based on research and experience.

We acknowledge all those who throughout our lifetimes have facilitated our personal and professional growth: parents, families, students, professors, friends, and colleagues. We include a special note of thanks in memory of Caleb Smith, long-time speech communication editor of Holt, Rinehart and Winston and a believer in individuals and in our discipline.

Denver, Colorado   FRANK E. X. DANCE
                                             CARL E. LARSON

---

[1] Lee Thayer, "Communication and Organization Theory," in *Human Communication Theory*, F. E. X. Dance, ed. (New York: Holt, Rinehart and Winston, Inc., 1967), p. 72.

INTRODUCTION

The field of speech communication is committed to the study of spoken symbolic interaction. One of its goals is individual self-actualization and the improvement of the human condition. Speech communication has a long history and an intense present. It is not just the study of dead speakers, or of learning how to make beautiful oral sounds.

The goal of this book, augmented by your teacher, is the application of theory to everyday practice. The book is meant to present a cutting edge. A sharp edge on a knife cannot be developed by drawing the blade across a soft surface—the blade must meet resistance, it must be honed against material of some substance. Similarly a mind, to be fully developed, must be tested against material of some difficulty. We make no apology for the rigor of the book's content—we have great respect for the quality of our college and university students. The book is meant to match in rigor the quality of today's student intellect.

For most of us the theory presented here has value only in practice. The practical demonstration of theoretical points depends on the application and good will of the student under the supporting direction and advice of an informed and experienced teacher.

CONTENTS

SPEECH
COMMUNICATION
Concepts and Behavior

Chapter 1

BASIC

CONCEPTS

OF

SPEECH

COMMUNICATION

1.1. Human communication has a practical history as old as man and a theoretical history of at least four thousand years.[1] Yet man's communication practice has seldom been visibly influenced by the available theory. Of course there have always been individuals who try to test or apply the theory, but most men have engaged in daily communication on a practical level while remaining ignorant of the theoretical statements which have been produced for the guidance of practical human communication. This reality does not alter the belief that practice guided by theory is preferable to practice guided by chance and tradition. There are some who are able to play a musical instrument without having received formal instruction, but most often formal instruction improves the playing of these individuals. Where a complex skill is involved, or where a relatively simple skill is altered by complex situations, instruction in the theoretical base of the skill should improve practical performance.

Just as some people successfully engage in practice with

[1] Egyptian writings from around 2500 B.C. offer practical advice for human communication. See Battiscombe Gunn, *The Instructions of Ptah-ho-tep and the Instructions of Kegemini* (London: John Murray, 1948).

little knowledge of theory, others know about the theoretical base of an activity but seem incapable of performing the activity itself. One may know all about basketball and be unable to play the game. One may know all about human communication and be a relatively unsuccessful communicator. Practice without theory and theory without practice both lack that element which integrates human behavior—the informed practical application of theory. The combination of "knowing about" with "knowing" often produces the most desirable result. Good theory, applied correctly, should produce good practical effects, and good practical effects are essentially relevant for man.

There need be no conflict between theory and practice. A true or correct theory will, if accurately applied, result in true or correct practice. The old accusation, "This is right in theory but it doesn't work in practice," should really be worded, "This is wrong in theory and consequently it is wrong in practice." As theologian Paul Tillich once commented, "There is no true theory which is wrong in practice."

This text is organized to present a firm theoretical base and then provide materials which will help the student to test the theory in practice. If the theory has any validity, then the student's success or failure in his practical experiences should be explained in part by that theory—but only in part, because no totally integrated theory of human communication is yet available.

The result of studying this text and participating in planned practical activities with the assistance of a trained, skilled resource person should be the development of an understanding of the elements of speech communication theory and the development of appropriate skill in the practical application of these elements to one's speech communication behavior.

Obviously, it is impossible to make a clear-cut distinction between theory and practice. Too often one shades into the other, and the line of demarcation is too deep in shadow to be clearly discerned. So it is with most concepts: seldom is the world of experience so clearly defined that we can always tell truth from fiction or right from wrong. Truth is a concept and fiction is a concept. Both concepts might have some things in common while containing other elements which in constellation distinguish one concept from the other.

1.2. In speech communication the basic concepts provide the student, whether he is practitioner, researcher, or a combination of both, with a way of interpreting his experience from a speech communication point of view. An individual confronted twice with the same set of experiences may organize those experiences differently depending on his conceptual orientation or his emotional state. What is threatening at one time is funny another. What is interesting in one situation is boring in another. Concepts serve as real, if unstated, rules for making observations and organizing experience.[2] An individual may have an emotional expectational set, and he may have a conceptual expectational set. The expectational set often plays a major part in determining what the individual sees. Two individuals with different emotional or conceptual expectational sets may derive entirely different impressions after exposure to identical stimulation. Expectational sets result in selective perception. How one perceives reality affects how one organizes and judges reality. Selective perception occurs when someone voluntarily exposes himself to material with which he is already in agreement and guards himself against exposure to material with which he disagrees or with which he feels he may disagree.[3] Selective perception plays a part in the choice, perception, and organization of available stimuli.

The concepts with which your mind is equipped play an important role in how you perceive, organize, and judge the stimuli available to you. Two scholars viewing the same incident taking place on a street might interpret the incident completely differently, depending on their academic discipline. An anecdote concerns a man who bought into a short-order restaurant business and called in a sociologist, a psychologist, and a communication consultant to examine the business and make recommendations for its improvement. All three consultants agreed that the problem centered around the manner in which the orders for food were handled by the waitresses and the cook. The sociologist counseled the owner that the problem was a sociological one resulting from the perceived

---

[2] Margaret J. Fisher, "A Metatheoretical Analysis of the Literature on Theory-Construction in Speech-Communication" (Master's thesis, University of Wisconsin–Milwaukee, 1969), p. 26.

[3] Bernard Berelson and Gary A. Steiner, *Human Behavior: An Inventory of Scientific Findings* (New York: Harcourt Brace Jovanovich, Inc., 1964), p. 529–31, A1–A1.4.

differences in social position on the part of the cook and of the waitresses. The psychologist told the owner that the problem was a psychological one resulting from differing self-concepts on the part of the cook and of the waitresses. The communication consultant advised the owner that the problem was one of a communication breakdown between the cook and the waitresses. Each consultant interpreted the problem in terms of the conceptual framework provided by his own discipline.

A concept is the result of a generalizing mental operation; once formed, it structures the behavioral field observed. The basic concepts of speech communication result from efforts to group together stimuli, observations, or feelings and then to name the group. The grouping is the concept and the name, or term, is the label for the specific concept.[4] The concepts presented here will be identified by the terms which have been generally attached to them.

The value of the concept lies in its usefulness in helping the student determine when there is and when there is not an instance of it. If the concept fails to do this then it "... may be criticized legitimately as being inadequately defined."[5]

It is important that our concepts retain a certain amount of openness to allow for conceptual expansion and shrinkage as we gain experience and understanding. The openness will enable us to keep our mind on the critical and distinguishing marks of a concept while protecting us from a commitment to complete closure, or specificity. Once a knot is pulled tight it is difficult to unravel it so as to see the different strands of which it is composed. With concepts, too, it is often worthwhile to avoid pulling them too tight.

1.3. When presenting basic speech communication concepts we have tried to create a family of concepts by progressively delimiting the field of applicable experience. Our move from the general to the specific reflects (1) the basic logical process of deduction, (2) the principle of emergent specificity, and (3) an effort to apply what we have recently learned concerning the relationship of uncertainty and information.

---

[4] Frank E. X. Dance, "The 'Concept' of Communication," *The Journal of Communication*, Vol. 20, No. 2 (June 1970), 201–10.

[5] May Brodbeck, "General Introduction," in *Readings in the Philosophy of the Social Sciences*, ed. by May Brodbeck (New York: The Macmillan Company, 1968), I–II, p. 5.

Logically you can move either from the general to the specific—deduction—or from the specific to the general—induction. The development of the scientific method has favored the inductive logical process. However, there seems to be support both from reason and from experience for the idea that deduction is a more basic and natural human process than induction. Lenneberg states,

> We are discovering a basic process that is reflected in language as well as in many other aspects of behavior. It consists of first grasping a whole that is subsequently further differentiated, each of the specifics arriving at a different time and being subordinated to the whole by a process of temporal integration. In productive behavior a plan for the whole is differentiated into components, and the temporal integration results in ordering of movements (or thoughts).[6]

The use of deduction in the presentation of basic speech communication concepts flows naturally from the inductive process generally used in concept formation. We move from the inductive formation of concepts, based on the observation and grouping of discrete stimuli, to the deductive ordering and application of these concepts.

The principle of emergent specificity suggests that we, as humans, generally develop control of an overall concept or organism first and then secondarily develop control of more specific parts or applications of the concept or organism. In the development of an infant's control over his own body we can see an example of the principle of emergent specificity at work. Initially the infant reacts to a stimulus with his entire body. If you poke him he cries all over, so to speak. He reacts by waving his arms and legs and wriggling his torso. As the infant matures he will react to a stimulus with ever more progressive discrimination, until eventually if you touch him on the arm he moves the arm and not the rest of his body. In like manner we can develop our control over the basic concepts of speech communication by first grasping the broadest concepts and then moving to specific applications of broad concepts or to more specific concepts.

Until the combining of work by Wiener[7] and Shannon[8] it was

---

[6] Eric H. Lenneberg, *Biological Foundations of Language* (New York: John Wiley & Sons, Inc., 1967), p. 296.

[7] Norbert Wiener, *Cybernetics: Or Control and Communication in the Animal and the Machine*. (New York: John Wiley & Sons, Inc., 1948).

[8] Claude E. Shannon, "The Mathematical Theory of Communication," *Bell System Technical Journal* (July and October 1948).

very difficult to measure accurately the flow of information. For that matter, it was very difficult to decide exactly what "information" was, so that it could be measured. Shannon developed a method of measuring information in terms of the reduction of uncertainty. He showed how one could make quantitative statements concerning information in terms of how much any given piece of information reduced the information receiver's uncertainty concerning the subject of the information. If you know that it is daytime and someone tells you that it is daytime, you have not gained much information, since what you have been told does not reduce much uncertainty in you over whether it is daytime. (Of course, you have learned that your informer also knows that it is daytime, and this is *some* information.) If, however, you do not know whether it is day or night and someone tells you it is daytime, then your uncertainty has been reduced substantially in quantitative terms. Thus information varies in terms of uncertainty. The more the uncertainty, the greater the possibility of more information. Information is a selection from uncertainty, and thus a reduction of uncertainty and an increasing of predictability. In developing basic concepts of speech communication we can successively reduce the degree of uncertainty and simultaneously increase the degree of conceptual specificity, predictability, and control. We can try to move from the broadest range of uncertainty through delimiting constraints to ever more conceptual control.

1.4. Terms, Descriptions, Discussions, and Examples of Basic Speech Communication Concepts

Conceptual Term: **STIMULUS** (pl. stimuli)

Conceptual Description. *A unit of sensory input, either internal or external, which rouses the mind; incites to activity; serves as an energizer, arouser, or activator. An agent capable of directly influencing the activity of living protoplasm (the agent itself does not need to be living protoplasm).*

Discussion. *It has been said that to a human infant the world is just a blooming, buzzing confusion. All of the multitudinous stimuli impinging on the newborn child must seem, from his viewpoint, to be without order or meaning. Stimulus (stimuli) is the broadest conceptual category from which all smaller units must be structured. Berelson and Steiner comment that the concept of a stimulus is a key one.*[9]

Examples. *Sounds, lights, air, seasonal fragrances, humidity, temperature, air pressure.*

Conceptual Term: **INFORMATION**

Conceptual Description. *A perceived selection or choice from available stimuli, resulting in reduction of uncertainty. The selection or choice may be either accidental or purposive.*

Discussion. *Information results when a stimulus influences to reduce uncertainty. Another description of this concept states,*

... information refers to knowledge that one does not have about what is coming next in a sequence of symbols.[10]

Information is not to be confused with meaning. Shannon's mathematical formulas measure quantity of information, not of meaning. Information is a narrower concept than the concept of stimulus.

Examples. *A particular light is perceived from many available light stimuli. A particular sound is perceived from many available sound stimuli. From all the sounds of a summer night one suddenly consciously perceives the buzzing of a mosquito.*

Conceptual Term: **COMMUNICATION**

Conceptual Description. *The process (or the product of*

[9] Berelson and Steiner, p. 87.
[10] Allan R. Broadhurst and Donald K. Darnell, "An Introduction to Cybernetics and Information Theory," *The Quarterly Journal of Speech*, Vol. 51 (December 1965), 442-53.

the process) of acting on information. Limited to or-
ganisms.[11]

Discussion. *Communication at the level of its broadest*
conceptual usage is not limited to humans but can be engaged
in by any living organism. Nor is all communication
intentional; the sender of a message may do so accidentally.
There need not be a satisfactory fulfillment of the sender's
desires for communication to take place. It is not necessary
to consider communication at this level as being either
"good" or "bad," "effective" or "ineffective." Communica-
tion implies activity. Since communication operates on
information, communication involves the reduction of un-
certainty. However, reduction of uncertainty is an attribute
peculiar to information rather than to communication.
Communication results when the organism acts upon the
information.

A few of the other descriptions of this concept state:

Communication, then, is an 'effort after meaning,' a creative
act initiated by man in which he seeks to discriminate and
organize cues so as to orient himself in his environment and
satisfy his changing needs.[12]

Communication . . . is essentially the *relationship* set up by
the transmission of stimuli and the evocation of response.[13]

In the main, communication has as its central interest
those behavioral situations in which a source transmits a
message to a receiver(s) with conscious intent to affect the
latter's behaviors.[14]

Communication is the eliciting of a response.[15]

[11] Earl W. Count, "Animal Communication in Man—Science: An Essay in Perspective," in *Approaches to Animal Communication*, eds. T. A. Sebeok and Alexandra Ramsay (The Hague: Mouton, 1969), pp. 71–130. Count, in this wide-ranging and interesting essay, suggests that only "Organisms quest for information; paraphrased, they exert effort after meaning. . . . The physical environment does not communicate. This is a corollary or a converse of the above" (p. 82).

[12] Dean C. Barnlund, *Interpersonal Communication* (Boston: Houghton Mifflin Company, 1968), p. 6.

[13] Colin Cherry, *On Human Communication* (Cambridge, Mass.: The M.I.T. Press, 1964), pp. 6–7.

[14] Gerald R. Miller, "On Defining Communication: Another Stab," *Journal of Communication*, Vol. 16 (June 1966), 88–98.

[15] Frank E. X. Dance, "Toward a Theory of Human Communication," in *Human Communication Theory: Original Essays*, ed. F. E. X. Dance (New York: Holt, Rinehart and Winston, Inc., 1967), pp. 288–309.

Communication is a narrower concept than information.

Examples. *Having perceived the buzzing of a mosquito, the person acts on this information to direct his behavior either to escape the mosquito or to slap it. Acting on the information constitutes communication.*
An eagle, soaring high above the land, perceives a small movement below (information); acting on this information, he swoops down on a hare. Acting on the information constitutes communication.

Conceptual Term: SPEECH

Conceptual Description. *A genetically determined, individual psycho–physiological activity consisting of the production of phonated, articulated sound through the interaction and coordination of cortical, laryngeal, and oral structures.*

Discussion. *Speech exists only in concrete actualities. It is tied to a specific producing organism. Although it can be developed in some species through training, it seems to develop spontaneously only in human beings. Other descriptions of this concept state:*

> In a restricted sense, speech is a medium that employs an oral linguistic code that enables one human being to express feelings and to communicate thoughts to another human being.[16]
> Speech is an individual physical activity which may be described as the manner of communication, distinguished from the means provided by language.[17]

Speech is a specific modality for the carrying of information or for the process of communication and is thus a narrower concept.

[16] Jon Eisenson, J. Jeffrey Auer, and John V. Irwin, *The Psychology of Communication* (New York: Appleton-Century-Crofts, 1963), p. 6.
[17] John B. Newman, "The Categorization of Disorders of Speech, Language, and Communication," *Journal of Speech and Hearing Disorders*, Vol. 27, No. 3 (August 1962), 287–89.

Example. *The meaningless sounds produced by a babbling infant can be considered speech.*

Conceptual Term: **SIGN**

Conceptual Description. *A stimulus having a fixed single and concrete meaning regardless of context. A sign may be either innate or learned. It often announces that of which it is a part.*

Discussion. *Almost all nonhuman animal communication consists of signs. The produced stimuli often reflect a total organismic state. Human communication also makes use of signs. Another description of this concept states:*

A signal is a response which is invariably made to a situation, if any response is made at all. It is invariable and unconditional in regard to the situation.[18]

Examples. *Thunder is a sign of the dissipation of heat in the atmosphere. Wet streets may be a sign of rain. Many sexual courtship patterns in animal behavior consist of sign responses.[19]*

Conceptual Term: **SYMBOL**

Conceptual Description. *A learned stimulus having a contextually flexible, arbitrary, and abstract meaning.*

Discussion. *Symbols are peculiar to human beings. The symbol, unlike the sign, is often affected by the context in which it occurs. The meaning of a symbol does not lie in that to which it refers, but is arbitrarily assigned to the stimulus by its users.*
Another description of this concept says,

A symbol is something that stands for something else.[20]

[18] Eisenson, Auer, and Irwin, *The Psychology of Communication*, p. 9.
[19] Hubert Frings, "Animal Communication," in *Communication Concepts and Perspectives*, ed. Lee Thayer (Washington, D. C.: Spartan Books, 1967), p. 297–326.
[20] Eisenson, Auer, and Irwin, *The Psychology of Communication*, p. 8.

Examples. *Almost all words are symbolic:* mother, justice, love, money. *Ritualistic apparel is symbolic: the academic cap and gown, the vestments of a religious official. Many gestures are symbolic: the "V" for victory sign, the peace gesture.*

Conceptual Term: **LANGUAGE**

Conceptual Description. *Systematized signs or/and symbols.*

Discussion. *Animal languages are systems of signs. They are a combination of innate and learned behavior. Human languages are systems of symbols and signs. Although the propensity for the development of human languages may be innate, the languages themselves are culturally determined and are learned. Human languages are capable of making reference and of predication. A different description of this concept states,*

Language is a verbal systematic symbolism.[21]

Examples. *The language of the bees is an example of an animal language.[22] English, Japanese, and Swahili are examples of human languages.*

Conceptual Term: **SPEECH COMMUNICATION**

Conceptual Description. *Uniquely human. The process, or the product of the process, of the fusion of genetically determined speech with culturally determined language.*

Discussion. *Current data suggest that speech communication develops in the human being somewhere between 18 and 24 months of age. "Spoken symbolic interaction is the central focus of study in the speech communication area."[23]*

[21] Joshua Whatmough, *Language: A Modern Synthesis* (New York: Mentor/The New American Library, Inc., 1957), p. 20.

[22] K. Von Frisch, *Bees, Their Vision, Chemical Senses and Language* (Ithaca, N. Y.: Cornell University Press, 1950).

[23] Robert J. Kibler and Larry L. Barker, eds., *Conceptual Frontiers in Speech-Communication* (New York: Speech Association of America, 1969), p. 18.

This concept is something more than a simple jointure of the concepts of speech and of communication.

Example. *The individual production of language is the omnipresent and best example of speech communication. When English finds expression in an individual's speaking behavior we have an example of the concept of speech communication.*

Conceptual Term: **SIGNIFICANT SYMBOL**

Conceptual Description. *A significant symbol is present when a stimulus to which an arbitrary meaning has been assigned assumes that meaning for both the sender and the receiver.*

Discussion. *The concept of the significant symbol was first described by George Herbert Mead.[24] A symbol can exist and yet lack significance in a particular communication setting—thus the concept of the significant symbol proves useful in analyzing communication.*

Example. *Mead says,*

The significant symbol is then the gesture, the sign, the word which is addressed to the self when it is addressed to another individual and is addressed to another, in form to all other individuals, when it is addressed to the self.[25]

The speaker who in delivering a patriotic speech uses symbols designed to arouse patriotic fervor in himself as well as in his audience is using significant symbols.

Conceptual Term: **RHETORIC**

Conceptual Description. *Purposive, intentional speech communication.*

[24] George Herbert Mead, "A Behavioristic Account of the Significant Symbol," *The Journal of Philosophy*, XIX (Jan.–Dec. 1922), 157–63.
[25] *Ibid.*, p. 162.

Discussion. Rhetoric *is a word much used and much abused. Since before the time of Aristotle rhetoric has been the object both of praise and of condemnation.*

Rhetoric is a special case of speech communication characterized by a specific intent on the part of the speaker. The speaker plans his speech communication in terms of his goal and for the purpose of achieving that goal. Obviously, the goal can be to the advantage of both the speaker and the listener(s), or to the seeming advantage only of the listener(s).

With the entrance of the concept of rhetoric into our speech communication conceptual repertoire we encounter value and normative criteria of "good," "bad," "rightness," "wrongness," "effective," and "ineffective."

The best known classical description of this concept states,

> So let Rhetoric be defined as the faculty [power] of discerning in the particular case what are the available means of persuasion.[26]

Examples. *A politician campaigning for election to public office is engaged in the use of rhetoric. A suitor courting his beloved is using rhetoric. A parent exhorting his child to good behavior is using rhetoric.*

Conceptual Term: **VERBAL**

Conceptual Description. *Dependent on symbolic content for meaning.*

Discussion. *Verbal indicates the referent capacity of words and the learning mediated through words in their symbolic aspect. Obviously, words may be perceived through modalities other than hearing. For example, you are now reading words.*

[26] Aristotle in *The Rhetoric of Aristotle*, trans. and ed. by Lane Cooper (New York: Appleton-Century-Crofts, 1932), p. 7.

Examples. *Printed material, spoken words, sign language where the sign stands for a word—all are examples of the verbal concept.*

Conceptual Term: **NONVERBAL**

Conceptual Description. *Not dependent on symbolic content for meaning.*

Discussion. *Stimuli are nonverbal when their effect is independent of any arbitrarily assigned meaning.*

Examples. *A blush. A feeling of nausea. (It should be noted here that an originally nonverbal stimulus can have an arbitrary meaning attached to it and thus become both a nonverbal and a verbal stimulus. For example, a blush, originally nonverbal, can be designated to stand for maidenly shyness, thus acquiring a verbal meaning as well.)*

Conceptual Term: **VOCAL**

Conceptual Description. *A stimulus produced by the vocal mechanism and ordinarily perceived through the auditory modality.*

Examples. *A spoken word. A belch. A scream.*

Conceptual Term: **NONVOCAL**

Conceptual Description. *A stimulus produced by other than the vocal mechanism, although sometimes, but not always, perceived through the auditory modality.*

Discussion. *There is today great interest in what is often referred to as "nonverbal communication." More often than not what is being called nonverbal would be more accurately described as nonvocal. Nonvocal stimuli can carry verbal meanings.*

Examples. *A gesture describing length, height, and so on. Cracking knuckles. The production of sounds by certain animals through rubbing of the exoskeletal structure, as by some crickets.*

1.5. Most of the basic speech communication concepts can be charted into a family of concepts as illustrated here. Figure 1.1 shows relationships based on the organization of this chapter. The chart is not a closed one—concepts may be added, deleted, or changed around as research, thought, and experience dictate.

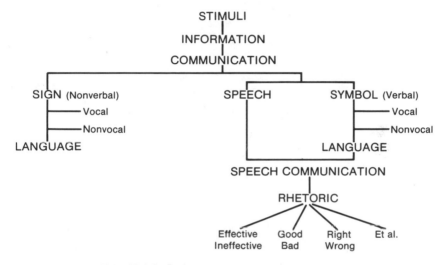

FIGURE 1.1 Basic speech communication concepts.

1.6. In presenting the conceptual terms and descriptions, we have tried to allow for an appropriate tension between flexibility and rigidity. Few, if any, concepts do not change with time or with additional research, thought, or experience. The object of setting forth these basic speech communication concepts is to enable the reader to establish a "set" for viewing experience in terms of speech communication.

Additional speech communication concepts, useful and basic but not needed at this stage, will be introduced where appropriate to the development of the book. For example, the concepts of "mode" and "modality" are described and discussed early in Chapter 6.

Whether the reader alters the conceptual descriptions will depend on his own understanding of the work that has already been done concerning a particular concept and on an adequate supporting rationale for the alteration he proposes.

SUMMARY

1. There need be no conflict between theory and practice.

2. Good theory, when applied correctly, should produce good practical efforts.

3. No totally integrated theory of human communication is yet available.

4. Concepts serve as authentic, if unstated, rules for making observations and organizing experience. A concept is the result of a generalizing mental operation. Once formed it structures the observed behavioral field.

5. The concepts with which your mind is equipped play an important part in how you perceive, organize, and judge the stimuli available to you.

6. The basic concepts of speech communication provide the student with a way of seeing his experience from a speech communication point of view.

7. A term is a label for a specific concept.

8. Retain a certain amount of openness in concepts to allow for conceptual expansion and shrinkage as experience and understanding are gained.

9. Conceptual descriptions may be altered if adequate support for the proposed alteration is provided.

EXERCISES

1. Select one of the conceptual descriptions in Section 1.4 and take issue with it. Support and argue for an alternate description (either in print or in some variety of spoken presentation). Where relevant, cite appropriate literature.

2. The chart of a family of speech communication concepts presented in Section 1.5 may be altered to show different relationships among the concepts. For instance, perhaps "language" should come directly under "communication" and before either "sign" or "symbol." Chart your idea of a family of basic speech communication concepts and present it to the class. Your chart may contain fewer or more concepts than Figure 1.1. When you present your chart, provide appropriate explanations and support for your suggested changes.

3. This chapter states that an individual's conceptual "set" can alter that individual's perception of the world around him. Identify several statements

reflecting your view of the world around you, in which you have considerable confidence. Think of several groups of individuals whom you might expect to disagree with your statements. On what do you think they base their disagreement?

ADDITIONAL READINGS

*Brockriede, Wayne E., "Dimensions of the Concept of Rhetoric," *Quarterly Journal of Speech*, Vol. 54 (February 1968), 1–12.

DeVito, Joseph, *The Psychology of Speech and Language.* New York: Random House, Inc., 1970. Chapter 1, "Speech, Language, and Behavior: An Introduction," is especially appropriate as another commentary on some of the basic concepts of speech communication.

McNally, James Richard, "Toward a Definition of Rhetoric," *Philosophy and Rhetoric*, Vol. 3, No. 2 (Spring 1970), 71–81.

Miller, Gerald R., *Speech Communication: A Behavioral Approach.* Indianapolis: The Bobbs-Merrill Co., Inc., 1966.

*Nielson, Thomas R., "On Defining Communication," *The Speech Teacher*, Vol. 6 (January 1957), 10–17.

Terwilliger, Robert F., *Meaning and Mind.* New York: Oxford University Press, Inc., 1968. A provocative treatment of the difficult but important concept of "meaning."

*Essays marked with an asterisk may be found in Kenneth K. Sereno and C. David Mortensen, eds., *Foundations of Communication Theory* (New York: Harper & Row, Publishers, 1970).

Chapter 2

BASIC

MODELS

OF

COMMUNICATION

2.1. The systematic study of communication is relatively new. The major bulk of the material likely to be labeled "communication theory and research" has been produced within the last three decades. Even so, you will encounter the term *communication* and its related concepts in descriptions of a fantastic variety of phenomena, ranging from the behavior of slime molds to the genesis of childhood schizophrenia. Similarly, you will encounter such broad definitions of communication as "communication is the discriminatory response of an organism to a stimulus."[1] In an abstract way such definitions speak of "life," for if an organism continues for long without a discriminatory response to a stimulus, we might be tempted to conclude that the organism is dead, or at least in a death-like state.

In Chapter 1 we stated that communication, at the level of its broadest conceptual state, may be regarded as the process (or the product of the process) of acting on information. Of course, in explicating the concept "communication" we cannot long remain at the broadest conceptual level. So, while we will argue that communication might

[1] S. S. Stevens, "A Definition of Communication," *Journal of the Acoustical Society of America*, 22 (1950), 689.

legitimately be considered the central social process, and that speech communication is its principal form, we do not pretend that communication, like God, is omnipresent. But if we wish to avoid constructing a theology of communication, we must develop a few very pedestrian descriptions of what is meant by communication, and how some scholars have chosen to view it in the past. Our approach will be to present some basic communication models. First, however, you should know that there is a multiplicity of basic communication models.[2] From the many that are available, we have selected five for purposes of providing an initial perspective. The first four have been selected because they represent "standard" basic communication models. You are likely to encounter them in any comprehensive treatment of communication models, because they were developed relatively early in the history of model building to explain communication phenomena. The fifth one we have selected because it represents a departure from the usual perspective from which model builders view communication. As such, the fifth model illustrates the variety of phenomena represented in basic models of communication. Second, you should know that there are many different kinds of models. The models we will present are predominately explicational [3] and taxonomic,[4] explicational in the sense that they attempt to clarify what is meant by "communication," and taxonomic in the sense that they emphasize the identification, description, or labeling of component parts of "communication."

2.1.1. The Shannon-Weaver model.[5]   An early model (see Figure 2.1) represented communication in terms of the direct transmission of information. The basic model describes an information *source* who creates a given *message* or selects one of the range of possible messages, and who *transmits* the message by generating *signals* which travel over a *channel* to be *received* and ultimately decoded by a *destination*. In speech communication, the information source (my

[2] See Ronald L. Smith, "Theories and Models of Communication Processes," in Larry L. Barker and Robert J. Kibler, eds., *Speech Communication in Behavior: Perspectives and Principles* (Englewood Cliffs, N. J.: Prentice-Hall, Inc., 1971).

[3] Joseph Berger, Bernard Cohen, J. Laurie Snell, and Morris Zelditch, Jr., *Types of Formalization in Small Group Research* (Boston: Houghton Mifflin Company, 1962).

[4] Robert Dubin, *Theory Building* (New York: The Free Press, 1969).

[5] Claude Shannon and Warren Weaver, *The Mathematical Theory of Communication* (Urbana, Ill.: University of Illinois Press, 1949), p. 98.

brain) creates or selects a message (that I have noticed and am pleased with the way she looks tonight) and transmits (by means of my vocal mechanisms) certain signals (sounds) which reach the receiver and are changed back into a message ("I like the way you fixed your hair tonight"). In this case "she" is the ultimate destination for which the message was intended.

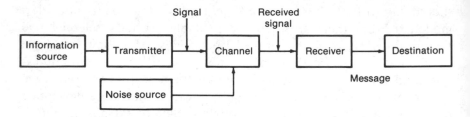

FIGURE 2.1   The Shannon-Weaver model.

Communication, as represented by this model, appears at first glance to be a relatively simple process. But consider just a few of the many things which might influence the accuracy with which the destination "understands" the source. First, I must select from an almost infinite range of available messages one which I hope will represent my feelings at that moment. Second, the message elements transmitted must be symbolically appropriate and the signal properties must be appropriate with respect to amplitude, intonation, and so on. If I transmit "I like the way you fixed your hair tonight" and there is a little too much emphasis on "tonight," the consequences might be very unpleasant. Of course, noise sources may affect the fidelity of the message. Environmental noise may affect the extent to which the message is heard, and semantic noise may affect the receiver's decoding of the message ("He doesn't like the way I *usually* fix my hair").

In the original description of the model, considerable emphasis was placed on the accuracy of message transference from sender to receiver. Some emphasis was placed on the extent to which meanings in the source and receiver approximated each other. Very little emphasis was placed on the consequences of communication for the behavior of the receiver.

2.1.2. The Lasswell model.[6]

> Who
> Says What
> In Which Channel
> To Whom
> With What Effect

An early verbal model, taxonomic in nature, is represented in a series of questions proposed by Lasswell as a general structure within which to analyze a given communicative event. Lasswell's model made explicit a concern for communication effects, and was regarded as an appropriate perspective from which to view mass communication, in particular. Criticisms of Lasswell's model, as well as a more elaborate communication model, are available in an article by Westley and MacLean.[7] The Westley-MacLean model will not be described here, but is recommended as additional reading.

2.1.3. The Berlo model.[8] Berlo's model is still probably the most fully explicated taxonomic model of communication. His attempt was to identify, label, and describe the ingredients which make up the communication process. Berlo's explication identified factors which need to be taken into account in understanding communication. Berlo assumed that communication is purposeful and that "all communication behavior has as its purpose the eliciting of a specific response from a specific person."[9]

One of the more important perspectives provided by Berlo is the importance of viewing communication in terms of relationships between source and receiver, with particular emphasis given to the role of the receiver in determining communication effectiveness. This is a perspective which we will emphasize in our subsequent discussion

---

[6] Harold D. Lasswell, "The Structure and Function of Communications in Society," in Lyman Bryson, ed., *The Communication of Ideas* (New York: Harper & Row, Publishers, 1948), p. 37.

[7] Bruce H. Westley and Malcolm S. MacLean, Jr., "A Conceptual Model for Communications Research," *Journalism Quarterly*, 34 (1957), 31–38.

[8] David K. Berlo, *The Process of Communication* (New York: Holt, Rinehart and Winston, Inc., 1960), p. 72.

[9] Berlo, p. 16.

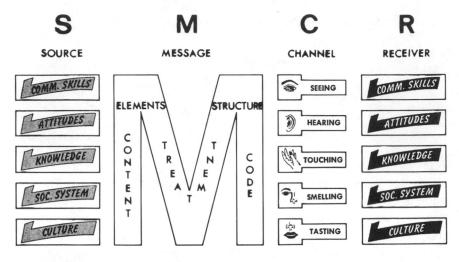

FIGURE 2.2   The Berlo model. From *The Process of Communication: An Introduction to Theory and Practice* by David K. Berlo. Copyright © 1960 by Holt, Rinehart and Winston, Inc. Reproduced by permission of Holt, Rinehart and Winston, Inc.

of basic communication concepts. Berlo characterizes the ideal communication relationship as a kind of empathic interaction:

When two people interact, they put themselves into each other's shoes, try to perceive the world as the other person perceives it, try to predict how the other will respond. Interaction involves reciprocal role-taking, the mutual employment of empathic skills. The goal of interaction is the merger of self and other, a complete ability to anticipate, predict and behave in accordance with the joint needs of self and others.[10]

2.1.4. The Fearing model.[11]   Another basic model, predating Berlo's but consistent with his perspective, is that of Fearing. Fearing's explicational model is based on the identification of four elements: communicator, interpreter, communication content, and communication situation.

Fearing defines a communicator as "a person (or persons) who produces or controls the production of a body of sign-symbol material with the intent (this term is discussed later) of cognitively structuring the field (or fields) of specific interpreters who are

[10] Berlo, p. 14.
[11] Franklin Fearing, "Toward a Psychological Theory of Human Communication," *Journal of Personality*, 22 (1953), 71–88.

assumed by the communicator to have specific needs and demands." Fearing points out that the interpreters may or may not be physically present (in the sense that you are not physically present while this is being written) but are nevertheless part of the "psychological field" of the communicator. The communicator has in mind, sometimes in a specific and sometimes in a general sense, an immediate or potential consumer(s) of the communication content. Fearing calls pseudocommunicators those individuals who do not originally produce the sign-symbol material, but who are somehow responsible for a subsequent presentation of it.

An interpreter is defined as one who "perceives (cognitively structures) a specific body of sign-symbol material produced by specific communicators as a stimulus field. . . ." The interpreter's perception of the sign-symbol material is conditioned by his needs, expectancies, and demands. Of course, part of the interpreter's perception is directed toward the source of the sign-symbol material.

Communication content is defined as "an organized stimulus field consisting primarily of signs and symbols produced by a communicator and perceived through single or multi-sensory channels." Fearing suggests that communication content "must be susceptible to similar structurizations by both communicator and interpreter." The communication content and the context in which it occurs are considered a "unified whole."

The communication situation possesses the "quasi-physical, quasi-social, and quasi-psychological properties which induce and determine the course of behavior of communicators and interpreters." The cognitive restructuring of the situation in terms of the produced content is presumed to be purposeful on the part of both communicator and interpreter.

As is the case with the proponents of the other models, Fearing goes on to discuss the dynamic interrelationship of the communication elements. For the moment, however, we are interested primarily in identifying and labeling elements in a basic communication process. The fifth and final model leads us to consider not only basic elements, but some of the simpler forms which relationships among basic elements may take.

2.1.5. The Baker model.[12] Baker's explication begins with two assumptions. The first is that man does not use language *in vacuo*. "If

[12] Sidney J. Baker, "The Theory of Silences," *Journal of General Psychology*, 53 (1955), 145–67.

he writes, it is that someone (known or unknown) may read; if he speaks, it is that someone may hear, even if he speaks only to himself." The second is that the general effectiveness of communication is very closely related to the degree of commonality between speaker and hearer. The hearer must be able to identify himself, at least partially, with what the speaker is saying. Similarly, the speaker must be able to identify himself, at least partially, with the hearer. Baker represents these degrees of commonality, or "reciprocal identification," with the two circles labeled A and B in Figure 2.3. Baker summarizes his first two assumptions with the statement ". . . that all speech involves a partnership and that this partnership rests on the ever-changing and highly sensitive basis of reciprocal identification. . . ."

Baker's next step in explicating his model is a marked departure from the models we have previously considered. Instead of viewing communication from the perspective of a relatively continuous flow of speech, Baker examines communication from the perspective of silence. He states that there are two basic forms of interpersonal silence. The first form of silence is represented by the S– notation in his model. This form of silence is called negative silence and characterizes a communication situation in which words or speech "break down." Communication situations characterized by negative silence are those in which fear, hatred, anger, acute anxieties, or the absence of any basis for reciprocal identification between speaker and hearer make speech useless.

The S+ notation in the model represents those communication situations in which tension is low, reciprocal identification is very

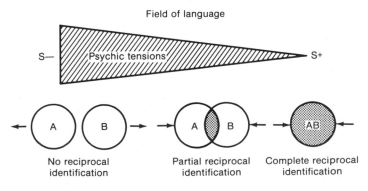

FIGURE 2.3   The Baker model.

high, individuals can remain comfortably silent in the presence of each other, and, consequently, speech is unnecessary.

The cross-hatched triangle represents the relationship between psychic tensions and degree of reciprocal identification between speaker and hearer. High levels of personal disequilibrium or discomfort, low reciprocal identification between speaker and hearer, and negative silence become diminished as we move toward the S+ end of the cross-hatched triangle. The major conclusion offered by Baker is that "The underlying (i.e., unconscious and unpremeditated) aim of speech is not a continued flow of speech, but silence, for the state of complete equilibrium, marked by elimination of intra-personal psychic tensions, is possible only when the position S+ in the speech field has been reached. This silence is one in which arguments and contention, whether expressed or not, have vanished, to be replaced by understanding acceptance on the part of the hearer (or hearers) and satisfied contentment on the part of the speaker."

All the models we have considered so far are basic. We have not treated them nearly as extensively as did their proponents in their original presentations. We have attempted to lay the groundwork for some subsequent conceptual refinements and distinctions. Later we shall consider some of the same conceptual and theoretical issues that are considered by most proponents of basic communication models. First, however, we need to introduce another concept which has become central in the formulation of more recent communication models. That concept is *feedback*. The question of whether the concept of feedback should be incorporated into any basic communication model hinges on whether basic communication processes are appropriately viewed (or ought to be viewed) as "direct transmission" or "interaction" processes. If communication processes are viewed as direct transmission processes, then feedback is not an attribute of communication; that is, communication can and frequently does occur in the absence of any feedback. In other words, I may encode and transmit a message to you without receiving from you any clues about the way you received and processed the message or its impact on you. On the other hand, if I view communication as essentially an interaction process, then I believe that the communication process is not complete until those who have participated in the production of communication content have at least had the opportunity to observe the responses of the receiver to that content. The second view elevates feedback to a more central position in explaining basic communication processes. Of the models we have summarized, Berlo's incorporates the feedback concept most fully.

2.2. Intentional and Unintentional Communication.

Those who conceive of communication as being intentional tend to believe that it occurs only when a source purposively transmits a message with the intent of affecting a receiver in some predetermined way. Those who believe that communication is or may be unintentional tend to believe that it frequently occurs in the absence of any intent on the part of the source to affect the receiver directly. That considerable differences exist in the way communication scholars choose to define communication can be seen from the results of Minter's survey of 150 members of the National Society for the Study of Communication (now the International Communication Association).[13] The individuals surveyed varied considerably in their preferences for intentional and unintentional definitions of communication. Some conceptual clarification of this issue is needed.

Let us begin with the assumption that, despite the word magic of the poets, the tree does not speak to us, the prairie does not sing to us, the birch does not invite us to swing on it. We may talk to ourselves about the tree. We may instruct ourselves concerning how we should relate to it. We may attach some particular significance to it. We may even project upon it or attribute to it some mood or sentiment. But that mood or sentiment is there because we put it there.

Now let us change the focus slightly to consider events or occurrences involving other people. Imagine that you unobtrusively overhear a conversation between two of your friends. You may attach significance or attribute meaning to the communication content produced during that conversation, but we could still reasonably maintain that these individuals are not communicating with you. You are communicating with yourself about them. You may generate and sustain a rich monologue, interpreting and reinterpreting, telling yourself engaging stories about what you are hearing. We may still maintain that communication is occurring on different levels; that is, you are talking to yourself while they are talking with each other.

[13] Robert L. Minter, "A Denotative and Connotative Study in Communication," *Journal of Communication*, 18 (1968), 26–36.

Let us approach even more closely the fine line which distinguishes intentional and unintentional communication. Imagine that while you are talking with another person, sitting and facing each other, you notice that the other person slouches down in his chair and just perceptibly lowers his head, his eyelids droop somewhat, and his rate of speaking begins to slow. You may "attend" to these cues, attaching significance or attributing meaning to them. You may tell yourself that the other person is tired, bored, uninterested in you, or characteristically emits those cues. Arnheim would label the cues "expressive behavior."[14] As long as these expressive behaviors are wholly unintentional on his part, and as long as he is not producing them as part of his communication content, then he is not communicating his fatigue, boredom, or lack of interest. You may talk to yourself about the cues, but you and he are not communicating with respect to them.

The conceptual distinction we are developing will be elaborated in Chapter 4. Presently, however, we need to recognize that communication may occur on different levels. The ways in which you talk to yourself and the ways in which you attach significance or attribute meaning to events and occurrences describe communication on the intrapersonal level. Thayer has stated that the basic phenomenon in all communication is "the process of taking-something-into-account."[15] So we may say that communication occurs, at least at the intrapersonal level, whenever an individual engages in taking-something-into-account, or, as we have stated earlier, whenever an individual acts on information.

If two or more individuals are engaged in taking-something-into-account, if that something is a sign-symbol content produced by one or more of the participants, and if some of the content produced by at least one of the participants has been produced for the purpose of somehow affecting at least one other participant, we may say that communication is occurring on the interpersonal level. If the communication content is produced by one and taken into account by many, and if the one producing the content is recognized by the others as occupying the central role or as having primary responsibilities for determining the nature of the communicative interchange, then we may say that communication is occurring on the person-to-

[14] R. Arnheim, "The Gestalt Theory of Expression," *Psychological Review*, 56 (1949), 156–71.

[15] Lee Thayer, *Communication and Communication Systems* (Homewood, Ill.: Richard D. Irwin, Inc., 1968), p. 28.

persons level. The more specific natures of intrapersonal, inter-personal, and person-to-persons communication are considered in Chapters 8, 9, and 10, respectively.

We are now in a position to modify our conceptual discussion of the term *communication* (Chapter 1, Section 1.4.3) in the direction of greater specificity. Whereas we have stated that communication may be either intentional or unintentional, now we may make some finer distinctions according to the *levels* on which communication occurs.

The following conclusions may serve as partial summaries for our consideration of intentional and unintentional communication:

1. Unintentional communication occurs most frequently at the intrapersonal level. Conceptual confusion in viewing communication may be generated by a failure to recognize that most accidental and nonpurposive communication may be appropriately viewed as special cases of intrapersonal communication.

2. Interpersonal communication may be viewed as *more* intentional.

3. Person-to-persons communication may be viewed as *mostly* intentional.

Further conceptual clarification of the intentional–unintentional issue may be obtained if, in viewing communication phenomena, we ask ourselves the question, To what extent is the communication planned toward some predetermined end? We could draw a continuum:

unplanned	planned
freely occurring	controlled
low definition of goal	high definition of goal

We could locate the three levels of communication in terms of where they tend to cluster along that continuum. Most intrapersonal communication would cluster toward the unplanned, freely occurring, low-definition-of-goal end of the continuum. Most inter-personal communication would fall along the middle range of the continuum. Most person-to-persons communication would fall to-ward the planned, controlled, high-definition-of-goal end of the continuum. We use the qualifier "most" because we can readily demonstrate that such conceptual distinctions as these can never realistically be absolute. You can easily imagine certain circum-stances in which intrapersonal communication may be planned, well controlled, and highly defined in terms of a particular goal. Someone may attend a private showing of a stag film with the very specific intent of being repulsed by the film and formulating and reinforcing many prior judgments about the film and the kinds of people who enjoy viewing such films. Similarly, someone may approach a blind date with a comparative stranger by formulating the specific intent of being highly attracted to that person, perhaps even with a highly defined goal of reinforcing the expectation that "this could be the start of something big." And of course, at the other end of the continuum, you have probably encountered many instances in which person-to-persons communication might more appropriately be described as unplanned, uncontrolled, with very ill-defined goals.

At this point we could become somewhat unconstrained in our thinking and allow ourselves to consider some interesting notions about communication. For example, we might speculate that individuals vary considerably in the extent to which they are dominated by one of the communication levels. You may have observed that some individuals exhibit extremely low variability in their behavior over a wide range of circumstances and social settings. That is, they exhibit a very narrow range of behaviors which remain relatively unaffected by markedly different circumstances and social settings. If circumstances change, social settings change, the behaviors of other people change, and even the goals associated with the social activities change, but the communicative behavior of one such person remains unchanged or exhibits extremely low variability, we might come to believe that he is dominated by his *intrapersonal* communication.

Another interesting speculation concerns individuals who seem to exhibit extremely high variability in their behavior over relatively narrow ranges of circumstances or social settings. These individuals appear to adapt easily and almost instantaneously to social conditions. Indeed, their feelings, beliefs, and orientations toward physical and social objects (in other words, what they say to themselves at the intrapersonal level) seem to be determined primarily by their companions or what the social circumstances call for. In special instances we may be inclined to label such a person "two-faced," especially if we find it difficult to understand his apparent disregard for consistency. However, we may be failing to recognize that the individual is dominated by phenomena occurring at the *interpersonal* communication level, and everything he says or does interpersonally may make perfect sense to him while he is saying or doing it.

2.3. Process and Outcomes. A fine line is frequently drawn between two "strategies" underlying the study of communication. Implicit in the *process strategy* is a focus on (1) explaining, and (2) what *is happening* in communication. Implicit in the outcome strategy is a focus on (1) predicting, and (2) what *will occur* as a result of communication.

Two things should be apparent to you. First, we hope that you see that the two strategies do not *necessarily* employ the same concepts or building blocks. Second, we hope that you see that we are not currently talking about the old theory-versus-practice argument. Both strategies are theory-building strategies. Dubin illustrates our present concern by identifying theories as tending toward power and/or precision.[16] Theories which tend toward power are explanatory; that is, they help us to understand phenomena. Theories which tend toward precision are predictive; that is, they provide us with a better guess of what is going to happen. Dubin notes that in the social sciences many powerful theories are not very predictive and many precise theories are not very explanatory. The same is often true specifically of communication theory. Some of our theories are attempts to explain while others are primarily attempts to predict. Again, this is not an absolute distinction but rather a conceptual distinction which we hope will help you interpret some of our subsequent discussions of speech communication. Subsequent chapters of this book will make it obvious that our principal strategy is a process strategy. Our major goal is to help you understand what is happening in and through speech communication and how the various functions, modes, and levels of speech communication alter what is happening. Occasionally, where the current state of communication theory and research warrants confidence in our ability to predict outcomes, we will inject such insights into some of the later chapters. Presently, to provide you with some perspectives from which to view communication outcomes, we offer Figure 2.4. Here are represented some outcomes traditionally focused on in the study of communication. These categories of outcomes are not exhaustive; they are simply representative of some major focuses in the field of communication.

The principal outcome categories we have identified are accuracy, influence, and social judgments. The criteria by which accuracy, influence, and social judgments are assessed vary with

[16] Dubin, pp. 5–25.

	Accuracy	*Influence*	*Social judgments*
Intra-personal	Approximations to "reality"	Attitudes, opinions, and beliefs	Self-concept
Inter-personal	Empathy	Attitude change	Attraction
Person-to-persons	Information acquisition and retention	Attitude change	Source credibility

FIGURE 2.4 Some outcomes traditionally focused on in the study of communication.

respect to the level on which communication occurs. In very general terms we may say that intrapersonal communication is accurate to the extent that what an individual tells himself approximates "reality." On the interpersonal level, we may say that communication is accurate to the extent that one person understands another's sentiments, preferences, values, and so on. On the person-to-persons level a perspective from which communication accuracy is often viewed is the extent to which information transmitted by a source has been acquired and retained by members of an "audience." At the intrapersonal level, the influence outcome is frequently viewed in terms of those circumstances or conditions which are instrumental in forming certain attitudes, opinions, and beliefs. At the interpersonal and person-to-persons levels, the influence outcome is frequently assessed in terms of the impacts of communicative exchanges on the attitudes of receivers. The third outcome category, social judgments, often focuses at the intrapersonal level on those circumstances or conditions which lead to the formation of certain kinds of self-concepts. At the interpersonal level, one of the most frequently focused on outcomes in the social judgments category is inter-personal attraction. At the person-to-persons level, some communication scholars focus on the circumstances or conditions which lead members of an "audience" to attribute credibility to a source. At the same time that source credibility is sometimes viewed as an outcome, many individuals focus on source credibility as a predictor of influence outcomes, especially at the person-to-persons level.

We introduce the process and outcome strategies at this point because we are convinced that individuals frequently adopt the unrealistic view that the study of communication implies one strategy to the exclusion of the other. Both strategies are important. We hope to help you develop an understanding of speech communication that is powerful and that will allow you to make some reasonable predictions about outcomes.

2.4. Design Features of Speech Communication. We have stated that we choose to view speech communication as the process, or the product of the process, of the fusion of genetically determined speech with culturally determined language. In the present chapter we have represented some basic models of communication, identified some simple components which make up communication, discussed relationships among some of these components, and presented some rudimentary perspectives through which communication may be viewed. We need now to provide some initial elaboration of the "speech" in speech communication.

Everyone knows what speech is. On the surface, the term does not seem to require much explication. But we believe that our understanding of basic speech communication phenomena might be facilitated if we reexamined some of the essential features of human speech. If you were asked to list a half dozen essential characteristics of human speech, could you do so? Think about this question for several minutes before reading on.

Now examine Figure 2.5.[17] It represents a noted linguist's attempt to identify the characteristics of animal communication (some of the characteristics are "human" ones, other characteristics occur also in other animals). Let us consider these characteristics briefly.

2.4.1. Vocal-auditory channel. Speech communication employs the vocal-auditory channel. Hence, individuals engaged in speech communication may simultaneously engage in many other activities either related or entirely unrelated to what is being talked about. The organs directly involved in the vocal-auditory channel are comparatively few, so that an individual engaged in speech communication can be simultaneously receiving many inputs which may either complement or interfere with the speech communication which is occurring.

[17] C. F. Hockett, "The Origin of Speech," *Scientific American*, 3 (September 1960), 89–96.

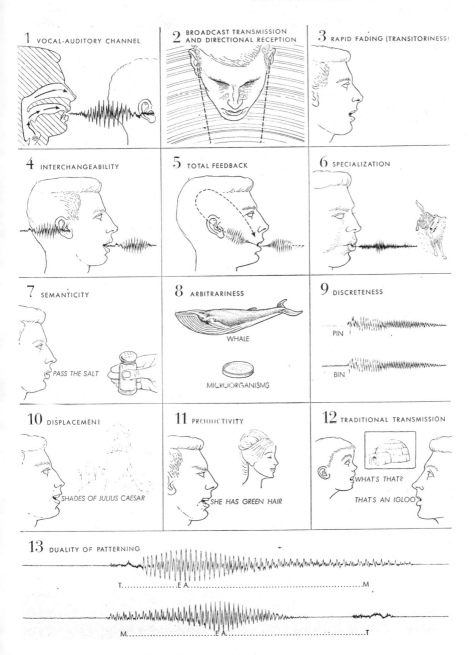

FIGURE 2.5 Hockett's thirteen design features.

2.4.2. Broadcast transmission and directional reception. Since speech signals can be "broadcast" it is possible to reach many receivers simultaneously. It is also possible to speak to one individual while intending the signals for the ears of another. Directional reception allows us to locate the source of speech signals.

2.4.3. Rapid fading (transitoriness). Speech signals, as they freely or normally occur, are transitory. The signals deteriorate as they are produced. There is small opportunity for backtracking, reflecting on speech content, or receiver control over the rate of the basic communication process. With written communication, you as a receiver can control the rate of signal reception. If you did not understand the preceding sentence you may reexamine it. Indeed, a week from now you may still reexamine it. But as speech communication freely and normally occurs you have great difficulty retracking and rechecking.

2.4.4. Interchangeability. An individual can reproduce vocally any speech communication content he has received. Often it is difficult, but it is generally possible. Thus, individuals engaged in speech communication with each other have some means for purposively maintaining similar orientations toward communication content. If you and I are talking I may purposively inquire, "Did I understand you to say? . . ."

2.4.5. Total feedback. While an individual is producing speech signals he is simultaneously auditing his production. He can correct his production; similarly, he can respond to his speech content in evaluative terms. Perhaps more importantly—and this is a point which we will elaborate later—the individual can produce speech content directed toward himself as a listener and may employ such a process for the purpose of regulating his own behavior.

2.4.6. Specialization. The individual may produce speech signals for the specific purpose of communicating. It has often been noted that the production of speech signals serves no essential biological purpose. When man talks, he presumably does so for the sole purpose of communicating, if not to others, then at least to himself.

2.4.7. Semanticity. Signals may be employed to refer to objects, events, circumstances, moods, or anything that is capable of being named.

2.4.8. Arbitrariness. The relationship between a signal and that which it names is arbitrary. Although some speech signals resemble that which is named, such as "howl" or "bang," the relationship between the speech signal and that which is named is nevertheless arbitrary. This point may seem terribly obvious to you. However, the next time the opportunity presents itself, ask a four- or five-year-old child the following question: "If we all agreed to do it could we call the sun the moon and call the moon the sun?" Prepare yourself for some interesting replies.

2.4.9. Discreteness. The speech signals we can produce and discriminate allow for such fine distinctions that we can employ a great variety of them, with corresponding fine shades of meaning which we can call forth in ourselves and others.

2.4.10. Displacement. Speech signals may be employed without reference to the immediate situation. Individuals can employ speech signals to talk with each other about things entirely removed from the time or the place in which the speech communication occurs. Indeed, man is probably the only animal capable of constructing for himself and others a reality entirely of words.

2.4.11. Productivity. Speech signals may be employed to generate concepts and thoughts that have never before existed.

2.4.12. Traditional transmission. Speech signals may be invested with meaning by convention, and such signals, with roughly similar meaning, may be passed from generation to generation. In our definition of speech communication we have noted that speech is genetically determined, but the language code which invests speech communication with "meaning" is culturally determined.

2.4.13. Duality of patterning. The sounds which comprise speech signals may be combined in a variety of ways, and the same sound elements, combined in different ways, may produce different meaningful signals.

Perhaps this review of the design features of speech communication has made the richness of the concept more apparent. Even if we ask about speech communication simply what are its basic features, we begin to discover the variety of things which make up the concept and the many forms it may take.

SUMMARY

1. The term *communication* has been used to describe a fantastic variety of phenomena.

2. Basic descriptions of communication are possible through explicational models of communication.

3. Most basic models of communication incorporate the concepts "source," "message" (or communication content), "channel," and "receiver."

4. Basic communication models may be distinguished as "direct transmission" models or "interaction" models on the basis of the extent to which the concept "feedback" is central to the model.

5. Communication may be viewed as both intentional and unintentional.

6. Communication may be placed along a continuum ranging from unplanned, freely occurring, and low-definition-of-goal to the opposite, represented by well planned, controlled, high-definition-of-goal.

7. Communication may be viewed as occurring on at least three levels: intrapersonal, interpersonal, and person-to-persons.

8. At least two basic theory-building strategies in communication may be distinguished: one which focuses on process and is primarily explanatory, and one which focuses on outcomes and is primarily predictive.

9. Speech communication may be represented as having at least 13 essential characteristics or design features.

EXERCISES

1. In small groups of four to six members, try to agree on and list six "attributes" of communication. By attribute we mean something which is true of communication in any and all circumstances in which communication may be said to have occurred. In other words, complete the following: "Any time communication occurs, the following six statements will be true."

2. Pick three different kinds of human communicative interaction (for example, small group discussion, persuasion, conversation, reading aloud) and then choose a model which you feel adequately accounts for the human communicative behaviors you have chosen. If you are successful in finding such a model, why is

the model appropriate? If you cannot identify a model, then what would you need to add to make a model appropriate?

3. Develop an original communication model specifically designed to explain or to predict outcomes in a particular social context, such as communication in dating, communication between boss and worker, communication between teacher and student.

ADDITIONAL READINGS

Smith, Raymond G., *Speech-Communication: Theory and Models*. New York: Harper & Row Publishers, 1970, pp. 14–25.

Westley, Bruce H., and Malcolm S. MacLean, Jr., "A Conceptual Model for Communications Research," *Journalism Quarterly*, 34 (1957), 31–38.

Thayer, Lee, *Communication and Communication Systems*. Homewood, Ill.: Richard D. Irwin, Inc., 1963, pp. 23–40.

Chapter 3

THE

UNIQUENESS

OF

SPEECH

COMMUNICATION

BEHAVIOR

3.1. The essential thesis of this chapter is that speech communication is a behavior uniquely human. Speech communication is not (not "will never be") found in any other form of animate or inanimate being besides man. This is neither a generally accepted nor a new thesis. Although we cannot conclusively prove the uniqueness of speech communication within this chapter, we must clarify our position, since both the question and the way you answer it affect how you view and value speech communication behavior.

When did man first develop the capacity for speech communication? Men have tried to answer this question for so long and in so many ways that the Societé de Linguistique de Paris in 1866 ruled that it would allow no paper on or discussion concerning the origins of speech. That solution is inadequate today. We cannot deny any kind of question in a time when many new investigatory techniques and ideas are being developed. Still, we simply do not know, nor do we seem to have the means of finding out, when man first developed speech communication. Speculation on the study of the phylogenesis (phylo = race, genesis = birth) of speech communication has taken varied and sometimes humorous forms.

Some theories suggested that language (note that writings on the phylogenesis of speech generally exhibit confusion between "language" and "speech") evolved when man imitated the sounds of nature. Those who proposed this notion called it the onomatopoetic theory, but one scholar, Max Müller, derided it as the "bow-wow" hypothesis. Other suggestions bear facetious names such as the "yo-heave-ho theory" or the "ding-dong theory." That the names of the theories are humorous should not be taken as evidence that either the essential theories or the concerns underlying the theoretical constructs are superficial or not worth reviewing. Some of the theories concerning the phylogenesis of speech are philosophical, some are psychological, some are physical and physiological, and some are metaphysical and religious.[1] At least one phylogenetic theory also bears sociopolitical overtones.[2]

Another approach to the phylogenesis of speech has been through examining the development of speech in the human individual. This method of examination is based on a hypothesis formulated by the nineteenth century German scientist and follower of Darwin, Ernst Haeckel. Discussing the relationship between the development of the human race (phylogeny) and the development of the human individual (ontogeny), Haeckel hypothesized that

> Ontogeny is a brief and rapid recapitulation of phylogeny caused by the physiological functions of heredity (reproduction) and adaptation (nutrition). An organic individual repeats in the short and rapid course of its development the most important of those changes of form through which its ancestors passed in the slow and lengthy course of their palaeontological development following the laws of heredity and adaptation.[3]

[1] The best essay available on the phylogenesis of speech communication is MacDonald Critchley's "A Critical Survey of Our Concepts as to the Origins of Language," pp. 45–72 in *The Brain and Its Functions*, edited by F. N. L. Poynter and published by Blackwell (Oxford, 1958). Theories on the origin and development of speech communication in the human race are also briefly discussed in G. W. Gray and C. M. Wise, *The Bases of Speech* (3rd ed.) New York: Harper & Row, Publishers, 1959, Chapter VII, pp. 455–72. For an interesting treatment of one approach to an anatomical theory, read Larry Wilder's research note "Genial Tubercles: Anatomical Basis for Human Speech?" which appeared in the "Research Reports" section of the *Central States Speech Journal*, Vol. XX, No. 1 (Spring 1969), 46–50.

[2] See "Speech Communication in the Soviet Union: The Phylogenesis of Speech According to Frederick Engles," by F. E. X. Dance, in *The Speech Teacher*, Vol. XIII, No. 2 (March 1964), 115–18.

[3] Mikhail Nesturkh, *The Origin of Man* (Moscow: Foreign Languages Publishing House, 1959), p. 20, quotation translated from Ernst Haeckel, *Generelle Morphologie der Organism* (Berlin: G. Reimer, 1866).

Haeckel's hypothesis, if true, would mean that we could trace the development of speech communication in the human race simply by examining its development in the individual. Without judging the value of the hypothesis in general, it seems invalid to apply it to the question of speech communication, since the contemporary newborn child is born into a symbolizing world in which speech communication already exists and already plays an important part in human affairs. Today's newborn child never has the experience of being a part of a nonsymbolizing world. On the other hand, during the phylogenetic development of speech communication (unless we are to subscribe to the theory of the divine origin of speech communication which suggests that speech communication was instilled, in its fullblown maturity, in man by God), early man progressed from ages of nonsymbolic existence into a radically new age of symbolic behavior. Whatever morphological changes took place, there had to be *a* time when the spoken symbol *first* appeared, and that instant confirmed a radical change in man's environment and behavior which occurred one time only, a change which today's newborn infant *shares* rather than experiences anew. We are unable, then, to describe or explain adequately the birth of speech communication in humans, but we need to describe and explain the part played by speech communication, both historically and contemporaneously, in man's behavior. Is speech communication simply a channel of communicating language analogous to written communication? Or is speech communication different in kind from all other forms of communication and found only in man? If the answer to the second question is "yes" then speech communication should be distinguishable from manifestations of communication in animals other than man. What do we know about the uniqueness of human speech communication based on research in animal communication?

3.2. In *Animal Communication*, Thomas Sebeok says,

> Man's total communicative repertoire consists of two sorts of sign systems; the anthroposemiotic, that is, those that are exclusively human, and the zoosemiotic, that is, those that can be shown to be the end products of evolutionary series. . . .[4]

---

[4] Thomas A. Sebeok, "Goals and Limitations of the Study of Animal Communication," in *Animal Communication*, ed. T. A. Sebeok (Bloomington, Ind.: Indiana University Press, 1968), p. 8.

In itself this statement is open to the interpretation that there are aspects of human communication which differ in kind rather than in degree from other systems of animal communication. In fact, the statement is not at odds with an interpretation of man's evolution as possibly being from a different evolutionary series than that of other animals. Professor Sebeok's point is that part of man's communicative repertoire can be directly traced to his position within the larger animal kingdom, whereas another part of man's communicative repertoire seems unique to man.

All animals communicate. Nicholas Collias structures animal communication in terms of the following situations within which communication seems to play a part: feeding, warning and alarm calls, sexual behavior and related fighting, parent–young relationships, and group maintenance.[5] Certainly man, as an animal, also operates within Collias's situations and communicates within those situations. What distinguishes the communication of man, within those settings, from the communication of all other animals? Certainly not that man makes sounds—so do many other animals. And not that man uses his body to communicate; so do many other animals. Neither is it that man communicates through odors, such as sweat, or through bodily adornments, such as scars and tattoos; so do many other animals. *The difference is that man communicates through symbols as well as through all the other means used by other animals.* All the means of communication other than symbols man shares with all animals. Symbolic communication is man's alone.

Although man possesses a unique communicative capability in his symbol-making and symbol-using capacity, he still builds his human communication repertoire on his animal communication history and proficiencies. Man, by being man, does not sever his animal origins; man's human communication emerges both from and alongside his animal communication. Recognizing and accepting this can help man understand the total communicative repertoire of himself and of responding others in his environment. Robert Ardrey, author of *African Genesis*, alludes to the value of man's recognition of his animal origin when he says, "The problem of man's original nature

---

[5] Nicholas Collias, "An Ecological and Functional Classification of Animal Sounds," in *Animal Sounds and Communication*, eds. W. E. Lanyon and W. N. Taylor (Washington, D. C.: American Institute of Biological Sciences, 1960), pp. 368–91.

imposes itself upon any human solution."[6] A denial of our animal origin and nature leads us to misinterpret some communication behavior patterns which, when recognized for what they are, can be understood and controlled. Why is a smile almost universally recognized and accepted as a gesture of nonhostility? Some explain this phenomenon by pointing out that an animal, such as man, can show lack of hostility by a nonhostile display of his primary weapon—his teeth. The "prickly" feeling at the back of your neck in an uncomfortable or unusual situation is analogous to an animal's hair rising when it is frightened or angry. Man can metamorphize his animal communicative patterns; he can transform them through speech communication, and this ability seems to be species specific. "Why is it then that chimpanzees cannot be forced to talk and that human children cannot be forced not to?"[7] Human beings seem to have the ability to use almost all of the behaviors available to other animals for communicative purposes.

But human beings also have communicative abilities not found in other animals. The zoosemiotic communicative behaviors seem to support the Darwinian evolutionary hypothesis of the evolution of man from a universal pool. In contradistinction, the anthroposemiotic communicative behaviors seem to be unique and discontinuous and thus suggest an evolutionary series unique to man.

> A purely Darwinian conception of the origin of language involved the principle that differences between human and animal structure and function are matters of degree. Animal communication thus could lead by insensible gradation to the faculty of speech in man. But the gulf between the sum total of achievement in the domain of animal sounds and human articulate speech is very considerable, and lacks a missing link. This strengthens the almost inescapable conclusion that some

---

[6] Robert Ardrey, *African Genesis* (New York: Dell Publishing Co., Inc., 1963), p. 13. In this fascinating book Mr. Ardrey suggests that man is committed to a self-destructive destiny and that only through mutations will the race continue. Although Mr. Ardrey treats animal communication extensively and perceptively, he fails to note that man, through symbolic speech communication, has gained an interior control which may well enable him to sublimate some of the more destructive animalistic urges and tendencies.

[7] N. Wiener, *The Human Use of Human Beings: Cybernetics and Society* (2nd rev. ed.) (Garden City, N. Y.: Doubleday & Company, Inc., 1954), p. 85. Serious questions are now being raised about the linguistic potential of animals other than man. See "Language, Name, and Concept," by J. Bronowski and Ursula Bellugi, *Science*, Vol. 168 (8 May 1970), 669–73. This essay describes the initial findings of an experiment designed to teach a young chimpanzee American sign language. It raises a number of important questions which research has yet to answer definitively.

potent qualitative change occurs at a point somewhere between the anthropoid and homo sapiens."[8]

What exactly characterizes this "difference" between human communication and the communication of other animals? The communication of animals other than man is bound to situations, is the result of specific responses to specific stimuli, and is relatively unvarying. Man's communication, on the other hand, can show remarkable flexibility, is often marked by the highest levels of abstraction, and is not situationally bound (within a given situation a human being is not always forced to exhibit specific communicative behaviors). These differences between the communication of man and that of other animals may be labeled differences between sign behavior and symbol behavior.

Thus, one way of characterizing the essential difference between animal and human communication is by saying that animals are limited to sign communication while man is capable of both sign communication and communication through symbols. If such a difference exists in reality as well as in interpretation, then it is impossible to assess man's symbolic capacity by examining other animals, which do not themselves share such a symbolic aptitude. Therefore we must move to work done mainly with human beings.

3.3. Ivan Petrovich Pavlov, the famous Nobel prizewinner and Russian physiologist, made a similar transition. He began working with dogs and gradually changed his research focus until at the end of his distinguished career he was spending more of his time dealing with human subjects. Pavlov did not use the terminology *sign* and *symbol* in discussing characteristics which distinguish human beings from other forms of animal life. He developed a schema of three signal systems (further elaborated in Chapter 5, pp. 82–84) to demonstrate how man builds on his animal heritage to achieve a uniquely human characteristic. Pavlov suggested that man alone is equipped to link together multitudinous stimuli by using a single vocal/verbal signal. He hypothesized that this unique human ability was the result of the presence in man of what he labeled man's *Second Signal System*. Pavlov made it clear that man's use of the

---

[8] MacDonald Critchley, "The Evolution of Man's Capacity for Language," in *Evolution After Darwin* (Chicago: University of Chicago Press, 1960), Vol. 2, pp. 289–308.

Second Signal System depended on the same physical and physio-logical laws that govern man's Sub-cortical Signal System and Cortical Signal System.[9] However, it is as a result of his use of the Second Signal System that man can develop signals of signals, or *symbols*. The phrase *speech communication* as used in this book has the same essential meaning as Pavlov's Second Signal System. Man's Second Signal System, or speech communication, allows him to use a single symbol to represent many sensory signals. The symbol is contextually free and is the essence of the process of abstraction and generalization central to studies of concept formation in human beings and to studies concerning the relationship of thought and speech.[10]

It has been suggested that man's language capacity and speech communication behavior are both "overlaid" functions, that man has no special organ for language or for speech communication, and that to produce language or speech communication man uses organs which have originally a more fundamental usage (such as the tongue for swallowing, or the larynx for impounding air). Recent research and writing have challenged the assumption that language and speech communication are overlaid functions. The general thrust of Eric Lenneberg's excellent work *Biological Foundations of Language* is that mankind has a species-specific potential for language which is based in man's nature and actualized in his nurture.[11] As Lenneberg says, ". . . it becomes quite clear that nature–nurture cannot be a *dichotomy* of factors but only an *interaction* of factors. To think of these terms as incompatible opposites only obscures the interesting aspects of the origin of behavior."[12] Although Lenneberg's "lan-guage" does not seem to be exactly the same as our "speech communication," the two concepts are closely interrelated enough for his conclusions to have absolute applicability to our interests. Lenneberg echoes, with evidence, Wiener's earlier quoted concern over why a chimpanzee baby cannot be made to speak and a human baby cannot be stopped. There is a biological difference with behavioral correlates between the chimpanzee and the human for

---

[9] These are laws essential to the neuronal structure itself, such as the law of strength of stimulus, the law of neuronal fatigue, and the law of neuronal summation.

[10] F. E. X. Dance, "Speech Communication Theory and Pavlov's Second Signal System," in *The Journal of Communication*, Vol. XVII, No. 1 (March 1967), 13–24.

[11] Eric Lenneberg, *Biological Foundations of Language* (New York: John Wiley & Sons, Inc., 1967).

[12] *Ibid.*, p. 22.

which, as Critchley observed, there is no explanation and which lacks a missing link that would support a Darwinian explanation. The human infant develops into a symbol using, speech communicating being; the chimpanzee baby does not. This seems to be true even when the chimpanzee baby is exposed to the same kind of environment as the human baby.[13] The explanation, then, does not seem to lie in nurture or environment as much as in nature or heredity. For "many modifications occur after birth in most vertebrates, but the scope of modifiability is always limited by genetic and prenatal events."[14] However, as Lenneberg carefully points out, we should not separate nature and nurture—we must consider both when we are considering the total being.

In a rich and closely reasoned book, philosopher Mortimer Adler turns his attention to the pivotal question ". . . of how man differs from other animals. Basically in kind or basically in degree?"[15] Adler sets forth certain criteria for proof of the question.

To support the answer that man differs only in degree the evidence must show that every type of human performance is found in other living things and in machines as well and that it is present either to a higher or a lower degree in man.[16]

To support the answer that man differs in kind, but only superficially, the evidence must show that man's objectively observable behavior includes certain performances not found at all in other living things or in machines; this must be combined with evidence that clearly supports the explanation of these distinctive human performances by reference to a critical threshold in an underlying continuum of degrees of either psychological or neurological complexity.[17]

To support the answer that man differs radically in kind, the evidence must show, as in the case of the second answer, that man performs certain acts not performed at all by other living things or by machines, combined with arguments that justify the positing of some power or factor in man's constitution that is not present in other things, animate or inanimate.[18]

[13] Cathy Hayes, *Ape in Our House* (New York: Harper & Row, Publishers, 1951).
[14] Lenneberg, *op. cit.*, p. 10.
[15] Mortimer J. Adler, *The Difference of Man and the Difference It Makes* (New York: Holt, Rinehart and Winston, Inc., 1967), p. 10.
[16] *Ibid*, p. 39.
[17] *Ibid.*
[18] *Ibid.*

Dr. Adler then examines these three possible answers. In Chapter 8, entitled "The Pivotal Fact: Human Speech," he states,

> Let me repeat: among scientists who consider the matter there is unanimous agreement that man and man alone uses verbal symbols and has a propositional language and syntactically structured speech. Included here are not only the biologists and paleoanthropologists who are concerned with the evolution of man, but also comparative psychologists, ethologists, and behavioral scientists generally (sociologists, cultural anthropologists); and in addition, experimental neurologists.[19]

Dr. Adler also considers the relationship of thought and speech as it refers to man–animal distinctions. Does the presence of speech communication in man enable him to think any differently from other animals? In fact, do animals think at all?

> Animals can certainly think, in the sense of learning from experience, generalizing, discriminating, and abstracting, solving problems by trial and error or by insight, and even . . . making inductive inferences from empirically learned cues or signals. The evidence is both plain and ample that they *can think in all these ways*. But it is equally plain from the observations of their behavior, in the laboratory or in the field, that they *cannot think in any of the following ways*: they cannot think about objects that are not perceptually present as well as about those that are; with regard to objects of thought, present or absent, they cannot make judgments or engage in reasoning (i.e., think that such and such *is* or *is not* the case or think that *if* such and such is the case, *then* so and so is not.)[20]

The arguments, summarized, state that man alone currently exhibits the ability to communicate through symbols structurally organized, and suggest that this observable difference may also be a radical difference in kind which in the future will restrict the use of structurally organized symbols to man. However, the arguments alluded to in this chapter do not generally suggest that any particular importance need be attached to the choice of modality (speech, writing, gesture, and so on) through which man chooses to

[19] *Ibid*, p. 112.
[20] *Ibid*, p. 136.

communicate through symbols. Such a position amply justifies the study of man's symbolic capacity and usage. We suggest that there is a further call to study specifically man's communication through the modality of speech, or speech communication.

3.4. In terms of its emergence in the individual and its impact on the individual's subsequent communicative development, the primary modality of symbolic communication is speech communication. Secondarily, speech communication may be translated into gesture, script, print, visual representations, or other modalities.[21] Man's interiority is expressed through the sound-making capacities of his zoosemiotic systems in addition to through speech communication with its anthroposemiotic origin. Indeed, rather than simply reflecting a static withinness, speech communication plays a formative role in shaping man's interiority. As, evolutionarily speaking, the hand is shaped by the labor in which it engages, man's interiority simultaneously shapes and is shaped by speech communication. [22] You simply cannot write everything you can say. Think how difficult it would be to write out, with all the nuances and innuendos, all that you have spoken in any one-hour period. When engaged in speech communication you may use such aids as a change in inflection, a certain way of wrinkling your nose or cocking your head, a change in pacing or in stress, all in the space of a few moments and often simultaneously. The spoken word lacks the linearity of the written word, and to transpose the richness of speech communication to the printed page is an almost hopeless task. We learn through speech to communicate symbolically through other modalities. The spoken word is central to man's communication; that centrality makes itself apparent in man's everyday activities. Words are not the same when perceived or projected through different modalities. A printed word often takes on an entirely different meaning when uttered by an individual. The simple word *no* can be made to carry an affirmative

---

[21] Walter J. Ong, S. J. *The Presence of the Word* (New Haven, Conn.: Yale University Press, 1967), p. 1. "Man communicates with his whole body, and yet the word is his primary medium. Communication, like knowledge itself, flowers in speech."

[22] The process of formation and information has been cited by Lee Thayer on pages 18 and 19 of his essay "On Human Communication and Social Development," prepared for the first World Conference on Social Communication for Development (Mexico City, March 1970), but flows also from a long tradition including St. Thomas Aquinas and Norbert Wiener.

meaning by the way it is said. The vast majority of human communication is carried out through face-to-face speech communication. This has been true historically and will be true in the future. Thus it is of the utmost importance that individuals, for their sake and for the sake of society, understand and develop their speech communication capacities. There is simply no substitute for person-to-person dialogue. Interpersonal speech communication is the most intimate and revealing form of human communication. Through their speech communication men construct themselves; through speech the uniquely human contributions to society have been and are accomplished. Speech communication plays such a major part in the shaping of individuals and society that it deserves and demands our understanding and a corresponding commitment to improve our use of it in our lives.

SUMMARY

1. Speech communication is a uniquely human behavior.

2. We do not know when man first developed speech communication.

3. Today's newborn child is born into a symbolizing world.

4. As Thomas Sebeok states, "Man's total communicative repertoire consists of two sorts of sign systems: the anthroposemiotic, that is, those that are exclusively human, and the zoosemiotic, that is, those that can be shown to be the end products of evolutionary series. . . ."

5. Man's human communication emerges both from and alongside his animal communication.

6. An understanding of our animal origin may help us interpret correctly some communication behavior patterns which arise from our zoosemiotic communicative repertoire.

7. The essential difference between the communication of man and the communication of animals is man's symbol-using capacity.

8. Man's speech communication capacity seems to be species specific and is not an "overlaid" ability.

9. Speech communication is the primary modality of symbolic communication.

EXERCISES

1. Some people (see John Lilly's book *Man and Dolphin*) disagree that man alone is capable of using symbols. Take issue with the statement that the use of symbols is restricted to man.

2. In small classroom groups, discuss the 13 design features presented in Chapter 2 and decide which are characteristic of human communication and which are characteristic of animal communication other than man. After deciding, compare your distinctions with those in Hockett's article.

3. Present some of the arguments against the primacy of speech communication and the centrality of the spoken word.

ADDITIONAL READINGS

Dance, Frank E. X., "Speech Communication: The Revealing Echo," in *Ethical and Moral Issues in Communication*, ed. Lee Thayer. New York: Gordon and Breach, Science Publishers, Inc., 1972.

DeCecco, John P., ed.,*The Psychology of Language, Thought, and Instruction*. New York: Holt, Rinehart and Winston, Inc., 1967.

Hoagland, Hudson, "The Chemical and Ideational Code of Information," *The Journal of Communication*, Vol. XIII, No. 3 (Sept. 1963), 174–82.

Staats, Arthur W., *Learning, Language, and Cognition: Theory, Research and Method for the Study of Human Behavior and its Development*. New York: Holt, Rinehart and Winston, Inc., 1968.

White, Leslie A., *The Science of Culture*. New York: Farrar, Straus and Giroux, Inc., 1949. Chapter 2, "The Symbol: The Origin and Basis of Human Behavior," pp. 22–39.

Chapter 4

THE

LEVELS

OF

SPEECH

COMMUNICATION

4.1. "Level with me!" "Is that on the level?" "I'm leveling." In conversation we often find the concept of a baseline, a level, entering our judgment. We presume that speech communication can take place simultaneously on a number of different levels and we seek to discern from which level a particular comment flows so that we may better evaluate it.

At first the newborn infant communicates in much the same way as all other animals—through motor discharge. Such motor activity, which is without conscious intent on the part of the infant, is interpreted meaningfully by the responding others in the child's environment. Through the interaction of the newborn infant with his environment— things, animals, and people—the infant soon develops an understanding—shadowy at first, but increasing in clarity with increasing age and experience—of himself as something separable and distinct from other reality. This experience is part of the initial development of a self-concept on the part of the infant and the consequent emergence of a distinct personality shaped by the interaction of the infant with his environment. Before the emergence of his speech communication the infant communicates on the same level as other animals. The importance of this animal level should not be underestimated, since it involves such basic competencies as the flow of messages through the organism's neurophysiological system. Disturbances at the animal level of communication, if severe enough, will hinder the full development of the levels peculiar to humanness.

4.2. Level I: Intrapersonal Speech Communication. On the first level sender and receiver are one and the same. Here is common-sense evidence that communication, including speech communication, does not require two persons. One individual communicates within himself; this self-communication may or may not be of that type we have designated as speech communication. In this book, however, the first level of intrapersonal speech communication is considered to imply the use of the individual's symbolic capacity either alone or in addition to the individual's other communicative competencies. In level one behavior both origin and destination of a message are within one person; the message uses internalized vocal symbols for the purpose of achieving and maintaining individual and social adjustment.[1]

Level one also aids in developing and maintaining a self-concept. The process of individual emergence involves the "informing" of person through speech communication. The newborn infant is human only in form and potential—not in actuality. What confirms the infant's emergent humanity is the process of interaction between him and his human environment. The infant links himself to this human environment through the development of responses to reality which are at the same time individual and universal. As they take on more of the characteristics of the responses of others, the infant's responses help him develop a sense of his person as well as a sense of the person of others. All this interaction is mediated through *communication in general*, insofar as the infant and all responding human others share basic neurological and psychological attributes with animals, and through *speech communication in particular*, insofar as the infant and the responding human others are specifically human and thus uniquely capable of communicating through symbols. Communication in general and speech communication in particular serve to shape the infant's internal view of himself and his surroundings and so to develop the inner form of the emergent

[1] See Chapter 5, Section 5.3.2, on inner speech communication.

human child. In this sense we state that speech communication informs the human child.

How the infant is immersed in symbols will affect his development, both physical and mental. Experiments performed on non-human animals indicate that the amount and variety of stimulation provided them materially alters their physical structures.

> At weaning age, one rat from each of a dozen pairs of male twins is chosen by lot to be placed in an educationally active and innovative environment, while its twin brother is placed in as unstimulating an environment as we can contrive. All twelve educationally enriched rats live together in one large, wire-mesh cage in a well lighted, noisy, and busy laboratory. The cage is equipped with ladders, running wheels, and other "creative" rat toys. For thirty minutes each day, the rats are taken out of their cages and allowed to explore new territory. As the rats grow older they are given various learning tasks to master, for which they are rewarded with bits of sugar. This stimulating educational and training program is continued for eighty days.
>
> While these animals are enjoying their rich intellectual environment, each impoverished animal lives out his life in solitary confinement, in a small cage situated in a dimly lit and quiet room. He is rarely handled by his keeper and never invited to explore new environments, to solve problems, or join in games with other rats. Both groups of rats, however, have unlimited access to the same standard food throughout the experiment. At the age of 105 days, the rats are sacrificed, their brains dissected out and analyzed morphologically and chemically.
>
> This standard experiment, repeated dozens of times, indicates that as the fortunate rat lives out his life in the educationally enriched condition, the bulk of his cortex expands and grows deeper and heavier than that of his culturally deprived brother.[2]

Remembering that it is sometimes dangerous to apply animal research findings to human behavior, in this case it seems that just as animal brains grow as a result of environmental enrichment, so also do human brains. Indeed, human brains increase rapidly in size during the first three months of life; the nature of the stimuli experienced during those first three months would be expected to have an effect on the rate and type of neurological growth.

The kinds of experiences a child has play an important role in his development both physiologically and psychologically. Self-concept,

[2] David Krech, "The Chemistry of Learning," *Saturday Review* (January 20, 1968), 48–50, 68. Copyright 1968 Saturday Review, Inc.

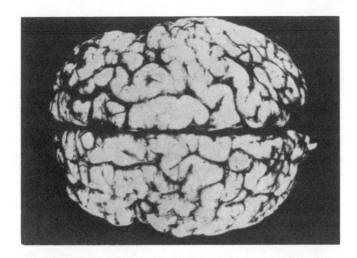

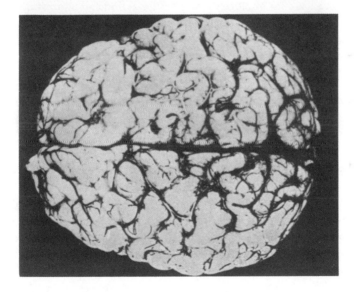

FIGURE 4.1 Photographs of the human brain at birth (above) and at 3 months of age (below) show its rapid postnatal growth. In this brief period of time, its weight has increased from 380 to 550 gm. Reprinted from Conel, J. L.: *The Post-Natal Development of the Human Cerebral Cortex.* Cambridge, Harvard University Press, 1939–55.

self-image, and trust all emerge in these formative first months, direct products of the quantity and quality of the infant's communication and speech communication experience.

All of us make continual use of the first level of communication; however, by the time we reach the college classroom all three levels are so intermingled that it is difficult, if not impossible, to specify on which level we are functioning.

The first level must be granted primacy of genesis and impact among the three levels of speech communication. It is the first to emerge in the development of speech communication and thus has the initial and most profound impact on the emergence of the second and third levels. Jurgen Ruesch, a leading psychiatrist who has thought deeply about the impact of communication on mental health, comments:

> The core of all psychiatric therapies is the improvement of the communicative behavior of the patient. This endeavor is based on the following rationale: 1. An appropriate view of self and of the world is the pre-requisite for intelligent and adaptive action and interaction with others.
> 2. Appropriate view of self can be acquired only if the functions of communication are intact and correction and self-correction operate properly.
> 3. If the patient never acquired mastery of certain aspects of communication, an attempt is made to teach those in therapy; and if his functions of communication are faulty, an attempt is made to correct these by somatic, psychological and social means.[3]

Dr. Ruesch suggests that all of an individual's communication with others is colored by his communication with himself. How one views himself—and that view is shaped definitively through communication—affects how one will communicate with others. In fact, if one's intrapersonal speech communication is sufficiently distorted, this distortion will be reflected, sometimes in pathological communication with other human beings on the second and third levels. For a readable and moving example of this relationship read *I Never Promised You a Rose Garden* by Hannah Green. An even more dramatic instance may be found in Helen Keller's autobiography.

The ability to manipulate one's inner world in a symbolic fashion seems to be essential to one's self-actualization. Unless one can verbalize his convictions, assumptions, desires, goals, and drives, it is

---

[3] Jurgen Ruesch, "The Role of Communication in Therapeutic Transactions," *Journal of Communication*, Vol. XIII, No. 3 (September 1963), 132–39.

almost impossible to measure their realization or to program oneself to enhance the opportunities and possibilities for their realization.

Our use of the first level is reflected in the frequency with which we "talk to ourselves." Almost everyone talks to himself. This activity has a number of purposes. First, we often talk to ourselves to let off steam, to ventilate our emotions. Second, we find that complex intellectual problems sometimes sort themselves out more clearly when we vocalize our thought processes. Third, we find that rehearsing a silent message aloud often clarifies our intent and highlights problems which would be faced in delivering that same message on one of the other two levels of human speech communication. We often talk to ourselves for the pure pleasure of it, just as we hum or sing in the shower—we play with our voices.

The multilayered reality of the self is most often displayed to others through the deceptively simple behavior of speech communication. Seneca said, "Speech is the skin of the self." Thus most of us are terribly sensitive to criticism of our speech communication behavior since that same behavior often either mirrors or protects deep-seated personal beliefs, attitudes, or feelings. An individual's attitude toward his masculinity or femininity is shaped by the speech communication which informs him and is displayed in his use of speech communication. Much of what passes for self-analysis or interior reflection is really intrapersonal speech communication by which we maintain communication among our various internalized roles and our multiple confusions. Indeed, mental illness is characterized by a breakdown in intrapersonal speech communication resulting in an incapacity to maintain communication among the various facets of individual being and eventually showing itself in a corollary incapacity to maintain satisfactory communication between the individual and outside reality. One of the characteristics of some great novels is their ability to show the interrelationships between a person's internal constructs and his external, social (or antisocial) behaviors. In Hamlet's soliloquies we share intimately in the intrapersonal speech communication of the leading character.

The process of speech communication is helical: it starts at the moment of conception and continues throughout life, moving in sometimes graceful, sometimes awkward spirals. The form and content of early intrapersonal speech communication affects the form and content of future speech communication. In speech communication it is impossible for output to exceed input. What goes on inside an individual manifests itself in his relationships with outside reality. Intrapersonal speech communication plays an essential formative role in the development of an individual's interpersonal speech communication.

4.3. Level II: Interpersonal Speech Communication. The second level of human speech communication occurs when one individual is linked with another in a communicative event. In level two discourse each participant relates to the other in terms of what sets the other apart from most other people. They take into consideration each other's individual differences in terms of the subject and the occasion. When one person gives another an order, instructions, advice, or asks a question, interpersonal speech communication is being used. Ordinary conversation between two people is also an example of level two speech communication. Happiness and sorrow, success and failure are often symptoms of satisfactory or unsatisfactory interpersonal speech communication.

What Martin Buber called the "I–Thou relationship" is the basic human relationship. Whereas the individual with his intrapersonal speech communication is the basic *unit* of human communication, the two-person or dyadic interaction is the basic *relationship* of human communication. There is no human relationship characterized by greater intimacy than an open and honest dialogue between two people. As Tavard observes, in such a relationship two people enter the interiority of one another. Your words, if accepted by me, enter the deepest recesses of my being. My words, if accepted by you, are given welcome, or at least entry, into your innermost thoughts, your past experiences, your plans for the future, your fantasies, and your hopes. Our mutual exchange of speech communication can effect both internal and external changes in one another's life state and life style. What other human experience is so specifically "human" and so completely intimate as the sharing, open, accepting speech communication dialogue?

Ordinarily when people suggest that a problem is one of communication or when they say, "That's an example of a communication breakdown," they are talking about problems which manifest themselves on the second level of speech communication. Second level problems are the easiest to notice but often the most difficult to solve. More has been written about this level of human communication than about either of the other two levels. When psychiatrists and psychologists seek to assist parents in achieving dialogue with their children they usually concentrate on second level communication. When diplomats and politicians seek to level accusations or assuage blame they usually concentrate on second level communication. Yet much evidence indicates that although difficulties and problems often display themselves on level two, their roots are in level one speech communication. The identification of second level as distinguished from third level speech communication is not always evident. When a number of people at a party are gathered in a group and talking together, usually in any given instance there are a number of interpersonal speech communication events taking place rather than a single person-to-persons event. The same holds true for most discourse in small group settings. In a discussion group a speaker is usually addressing himself to one other member of the group *specifically*, even if the speaker intends his remarks to be heard by the other group members *generally*. Even in these instances we should remember that the very presence of others during an interpersonal speech communication event will usually have an effect on the dialogue.

4.4. Level III: Person-to-Persons Speech Communication. Courses in public speaking generally concentrate on the third level of human speech communication. When one person engages in speech communication with a group of other people he is involved in third level speech communication behavior. When one individual speaks to others, concentrating more on what they have in common rather than what differentiates one from another, he is involved in person-to-persons speech communication. Whereas in level two discourse the participants relate to each other in terms of what sets each other apart from most other people, in level three discourse the speaker relates to his audience in terms of commonalities.

The communication of an individual with a group can be extended by means of the mass media. The press, radio, television, and film are technologies for the rapid transmission of messages to great numbers of individuals. Through such mass communication media, although the message is transmitted quickly and in quantity it is still perceived or consumed by individuals. Yet research in the psychology of group behavior tends to show that an individual's behavior is often changed by virtue of his being a member of a specific group or by being in a group or crowd at the time of message reception. In addition, the nature of the medium may itself affect the message.

Man achieves many of his objectives through cooperation with others. Cooperation requires communication; to achieve cooperation on the part of many individuals requires communication to many individuals. In light of available time and energy it becomes necessary to reach numbers of individuals at the same time, either by massing the individuals together and speaking to them all at the same time, or by massing the messages and making them available to many individuals at the time and place most convenient for them. Third level communication concerns itself with both these means of giving one individual the opportunity to use speech in communicating with groups of other individuals.

4.5. Interrelationships among levels of speech communication. Although the concept of the dynamic interrelationships among the levels of speech communication has not been specially treated in textbooks in the field, it is not new. Over 75 years ago Oliver Wendell Holmes, in his treatment of the autocrat of the breakfast table, hinted at this very concept.

> It is not easy, at the best, for two persons talking together to make the most of each other's thoughts, there are so many of them.
>
> (The company looked as if they wanted an explanation.)
>
> When John and Thomas, for instance, are talking together, it is natural enough that among the six there should be more or less confusion and misapprehension.
>
> (Our landlady turned pale;—no doubt she thought there was a screw loose in my intellects;—and that involved the probable loss of a boarder.)
>
> I think, I said, I can make it plain . . . that there are at least six personalities distinctly to be recognized as taking part in that dialogue between John and Thomas.

Three Johns {
1. The real John; known only to his Maker.
2. John's ideal John; never the real one, and often very unlike him.
3. Thomas's ideal John; never the real John, nor John's John, but often very unlike either.
}

Three Thomases
{
1. The real Thomas.
2. Thomas's ideal Thomas.
3. John's ideal Thomas.[4]
}

When we speak on either the second or the third level, our first level speech communication is visible. The levels are cumulative. There is no such thing as second level speech communication devoid of any influence from the first level, or of third level speech communication devoid of first and second level influences. The levels are not one *or* two *or* three, but rather one *plus* two *plus* three.

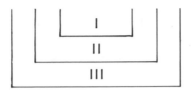

The additive or cumulative nature of
levels of speech communication

In the beginning the influence of levels on each other begins with level one, thence to level two, and finally to level three. Once all three levels have emerged, the interrelationship becomes reciprocal in that the direction of influence among the levels can go either way—from one to two to three or from three to two to one.

I. Intrapersonal

II. Interpersonal

III. Person-to-Persons

The levels are dynamically
interrelated after their emergence.

The kinds of constraints, blockages, and warps that an individual may develop on the first level will ordinarily show themselves when that individual engages in second or third level behaviors. Adolph Hitler had many intrapersonal problems and was often a paranoid second level speech communicator. As Hitler came under mounting

---

[4] Oliver Wendell Holmes, *The Autocrat of the Breakfast Table* (Boston: Houghton Mifflin Company, 1892), pp. 53–54.

pressures toward the end of the war, his third level behavior became increasingly erratic—mirroring rapidly disintegrating second and first level speech communication.

The levels constitute a kind of system, interrelated, mutually reinforcing, and mutually destructive. Consistently unhappy experiences on the second level can eventually disrupt first level behavior. The youngster whose parents constantly call him "stupid" may well begin to think of himself as stupid and thus create a self-fulfilling prophecy. On the other hand, reinforcement on the third level may produce increased self-confidence in both second and first level speech communication.

Remember that the three levels are dynamically interrelated and that the individual who is striving for healthy and effective speech communication needs to be aware of his behavior on all three levels.

SUMMARY

1. Speech communication develops and is manifested on three levels.

2. The levels of speech communication are interrelated.

3. The first level is intrapersonal speech communication.

4. The second level is interpersonal speech communication.

5. In level two discourse the participants relate to each other in terms of what sets each other apart from most other people.

6. The third level is person-to-persons speech communication.

7. In level three discourse the speaker communicates with his audience in terms of what the individual audience members have in common with one another to which the speaker can also relate.

8. The levels are additive and cumulative.

9. Although in the beginning the first level has the greatest impact by virtue of primacy of genesis, when all levels have developed they are then dynamically interrelated.

EXERCISES

1. Read Robert Browning's poem "Soliloquy of the Spanish Cloister" and prepare a brief report indicating the levels of speech communication involved, their location within the poem, and their interrelationship. What effect does the

first level have on the second level speech communication of the Brother who is speaking?

2. Read Chapter 15 of the Report of the National Advisory Commission on Civil Disorders (New York: Bantam Books #Z4273, 1968). Analyze the part played by third level speech communication in the incidents detailed in the chapter.

3. Analyze your interpersonal speech communication in terms of your intrapersonal speech communication.

4. Read Edward Albee's *Who's Afraid of Virginia Woolf*. How does Martha and George's level one speech communication affect their level two speech communication behaviors? Now reverse the question—how do their second level behaviors affect their first level behaviors?

5. The interrelationships among the levels of speech communication in your life may become more evident as a result of the following situations:
a. You have become aware of your impending death. There is nothing you can do to avoid it. You have the opportunity of giving one last speech to tell others what has been most important to you in your life; what you would avoid if you had it to live over; what you would do more of, had you the opportunity.
b. The end of the world is coming. Prepare a speech telling how you would spend your last day.
c. Across generations communication concerning sex education has usually failed. Why? How can this failure be overcome?
d. Because of a massive power failure your community is isolated: there is no radio, television, or movies. There are no papers. You must spend your time reading. You have enough time to read four books—what would they be and why?

ADDITIONAL READINGS

Barker, Larry L., and Gordon Wiseman, "A Model of Intrapersonal Communication," in *Journal of Communication*, Vol. XVI, No. 3 (September 1966), 172–79.

Ruesch, Jurgen, and Gregory Bateson, *Communication: The Social Matrix of Psychiatry*. New York: W. W. Norton & Co., Inc., 1951.

Rosenblith, Walter A., ed., *Sensory Communication*. Cambridge, Mass.: The M.I.T. Press, 1961.

Borden, George, Richard Gregg, and Theodore Grove, *Speech Behavior and Human Interaction*. Englewood Cliffs, N. J.: Prentice-Hall, Inc., 1969. Especially Part I.

Chapter 5

THE

FUNCTIONS

OF

SPEECH

COMMUNICATION

5.1. There are as many reasons for studying speech communication as there are people. Some individuals turn their attention to speech communication because of their desire to charm others through the medium of conversation. Others are interested in learning to be persuasive for reasons of pecuniary or political gain. It is not our intention to suggest a hierarchy of motivation in the study of this discipline. Rather, we hope to suggest that all the individual needs which are manifested in numerous reasons for studying speech communication are actually special instances of three basic speech communication functions.

Jerome Bruner, the eminent educational psychologist, has pointed out that it is "... necessary for the various fields of learning to assess the manner in which they contribute to the amplification of mind—the way of doing or of experiencing or rationating that is integral to them and that should be part of the way of mind of an educated member of the culture."[1] Bruner's statement is easily paraphrased into perplexing but important questions. What is the

[1] Jerome S. Bruner, *Toward a Theory of Instruction* (Cambridge, Mass.: Belknap/Harvard University Press, 1966), p. 38.

unique content of speech communication? In what unique manner does speech communication assist in amplifying mind and being? Is there a way of doing and of experiencing that is integral to those interested in speech communication and that must be a part of the way of mind of an educated human being?

Any college student should feel that the time he devotes to a subject is well spent. Students have the right to be asked to concern themselves not with trivia, but with matters of personal and social importance. The years available for devotion to study *qua* study are few enough that they should not be squandered on courses or subjects of dubious value. Bruner's comments, mentioned above, and the questions developed from those comments seem to offer a reasonable means of assessing the value of a subject. Let us see if the field of speech communication can answer them satisfactorily.

What we want to know is, do speech communication and the study of speech communication do things to and for the human being that are not done by other subjects. Can we get anything special or unique from understanding speech communication, or are we just spending our time on pretty but superficial social graces and personality frills?

Our argument is that speech communication functions so importantly in the life of a human being that the understanding and study of speech communication are at the very core of a liberal education. The word *function* is used here with a specific meaning. A relationship wherein one quality is so related to another quality that it is dependent on and varies with it is one aspect of "function." Another aspect is the lack of need for "intention" in function and the idea that a function is a consequence of some kind which may be anticipated and may even be, on theoretical grounds, logically necessary.[2]

5.2. Function is different from purpose. A function happens as an inevitable and natural result of something, while a purpose is that which can be done *with* something. For example, the production of heat is the inevitable result of the dissipation of energy. Therefore, the production of heat is a function of the dissipation of energy. The heat thus created can be used for a multitude of purposes: for

---

[2] See "Function," *Dictionary of the Social Sciences*, J. Gould and W. L. Kalb, eds. (New York: The Free Press, 1964), pp. 277–79.

creating personal warmth, as a source of energy, for melting ice, for making steel, for melting glass, and so on. Melting ice is not a function of heat since heat can be present without ice. But energy cannot be dissipated without the creation of heat; therefore, the production of heat is a function, not a purpose, of the dissipation of energy.

A vast literature is concerned with the purposes to which speech communication may be put. The traditions of classical and contemporary rhetoric often classify the purposes of speech communication as informing, entertaining, and persuading. These purposes appear in different permutations; some list convincing subordinate to persuasion, some include stimulating as a separate purpose, and still others consider actuating as a general purpose of speech communication.

Any of these goals may be considered purposes since they are the product of the individual's conscious or unconscious intent. However, they are not functions as we are using the concept, since they are not inevitable and natural results of the speech communication behavior of the individual. Later you will have occasion to consider the relationships between the functions, the modes, and the purposes of speech communication. Here, however, our interest centers on the functions.

5.3. Speech communication has three functions: (1) the linking of the individual with his environment, (2) the development of higher mental processes, and (3) the regulation of behavior. These three functions are independent of volition for their inception, although they are capable of being enhanced by conscious effort either by oneself or by others for oneself. They occur as an inevitable and natural result of the presence of speech communication in the human being.

Although we present only three functions here, we do not mean to intimate that there are *only* three functions of speech communication, but rather that only three functions have thus far been sufficiently isolated to warrant statement and adequately supported to warrant belief.

5.3.1. Function 1: The linking of the individual with his environment. As in so many cases where a statement seems obvious, support for the first function is especially difficult to gather and assess. Since we do not suggest that you accept the functions either as axioms or as assumptions, support must at best be probative and at least be so highly sufficient as to induce a strong predisposition in favor of acceptance of the function.

Colin Cherry points out,

> There has been speculation as to whether a fundamental difference between a living and a dead organism, in scientific terms at least, is that the former constantly reduces its entropy (increases organization) at the expense of that of its environment; here, entropy is identified with information which the living creature is constantly taking in.[3]

Indeed, the reduction of randomness, the reduction of uncertainty, the reduction of entropy may be the basic life function. Perhaps that is what life is all about—making order out of chaos. The essence of life is the gathering around a nucleus of those things which will sustain the organized form. At death the life-form again lapses into the disorganization which was its pre-living state. The means by which the disorder surrounding the striving life-form may be ordered and structured into nutrient matrices are the transformation of energy, the processing of information, and communication. Communication, human communication, and speech communication are ever more specific means of introducing form into the formlessness of the being emerging from nothingness into humanness. This process is obviously one of establishing relationships between the individual and his environment. In the following quotation we can trace entropic reduction from infrahuman biological systems through the uniqueness of speech communication.

> One fundamental property of human language that is shared by all biological communication systems is that of information exchange. Biological systems demonstrate the ability to exchange information between parts of the system as well as between the system as a whole and its physical and social environment. In the case of the human, it is quite as necessary that respiratory center neurones be informed about the carbon dioxide concentration of the blood as it is that ideas be transmitted from one person to another. This spectrum of information-exchange capabilities can be vastly expanded at both ends, for at one extreme we appreciate that subcomponents of single cells transfer

[3] Colin Cherry, *On Human Communication* (2nd ed.), Science Editions (New York: John Wiley & Sons, Inc., 1961), p. 59.

information and at the other extreme we appreciate that man possesses communicative capabilities that permit the construction of cosmologies. I am suggesting that language function be considered as part of a broad continuum of information-exchange operations that function to regulate and integrate biological activity, that the key to understanding the biological origin of communication systems resides in appreciating that all categories of biological activity generate specific information requirements, and that communication systems provide specialized capabilities for receiving, processing, and transmitting biologically essential information. This point of view suggests that communication systems evolve in specific forms in order optimally to meet specific needs for information transfer necessary for the preservation, growth, and development of an organism.[4]

In this quotation, as in others throughout this text, pay careful attention to the different terms and referents which appear. From time to time you may wish to consult Chapter 1 to refresh your memory concerning vocabulary and taxonomy.

Russian researchers, taking their cue from the pioneering work of Pavlov, often discuss the relationships existing between man, his nervous system, speech communication, and man's intrapersonal and social linkages. Pavlov examined the role played by the human cortex in enabling the individual to acquire and create new connections with his environment.[5] He went on to write of the function of speech in cortical linkages. In this regard, he suggested that speech communication signified a new principle in the activity of the cerebral hemispheres and that speech and speech communication represented abstractions from reality, making generalizations possible and thus constituting our specifically human, higher thinking.[6]

We start by discussing the first function in the earliest stages of human development because it is often clearer in these early stages and more easily separated from the other functions with which it becomes more and more intertwined as the individual grows older.

Function one is humanly socializing but essentially non-normative; that is, no value judgments are either stated or implied: no "good," "bad," or "better," no "worse," "right," or "wrong."

[4] Richard Allen Chase, "Evolutionary Aspects of Language Development and Function," in *The Genesis of Language*, eds. Frank Smith and George A. Miller (Cambridge, Mass.: The M.I.T. Press, 1966), pp. 253–54.

[5] D. B. Elkohin, "The Physiology of Higher Nervous Activity and Child Psychology," in *Sovetskay Pedagogika*, No. 11 (1951), 48.

[6] Ivan Pavlov, *Selected Works*, pp. 262, 285. Quoted in Elkohin, *op. cit.*, pp. 48–49.

If the first function occurs then one would expect that if speech communication were totally absent in an infant or child, the child would be incapable of forming a peculiarly human link with his environment. If the individual was deficient in speech communication there would be a corresponding decrement in his link with his environment.

In addition, the function suggests that environmental changes would also affect the individual's linkage. So we can examine three dimensions: first, the individual's own speech communication; second, the environment into which the individual is thrust; and third, the connection between the individual and his environment. If the first function is true then alterations in any of these dimensions should manifest themselves in alterations in the child's link with his environment. Since it is unacceptable to use human beings in experiments designed to prove the foregoing statement at the risk of severely damaging the individual throughout his life, we must rely on case studies resulting from accident or circumstance.

An individual's speech communication can be severely retarded by any of many problems, such as deafness or brain damage. The literature concerning the deaf, although ambiguous on many points, is absolutely unanimous in saying that deafness negatively affects the individual's relationships with his environment and with others. Helen Keller's youth, as portrayed in *The Miracle Worker*, testifies to the difficulties encountered by the deaf in their efforts to relate to themselves and to others.

Those unfortunate enough to have suffered congenital brain damage resulting in speech communication incapacities also experience difficulty in forming relationships, caused by decrements in speech communication.

An infant (note that the very word *infant* is derived from "in," meaning *without*, and "fari," meaning *speech*) is born into a world of things nonsymbolic and things symbolic. It is false to suggest that he is born into a world of "real" things and a world of symbols, since symbols are fully as real as other forms of reality.

A baby is born. It is a wriggling mass of cytoplasm inclosed in membranous tissues tying together and creating the distinguishable form of a human being. It is physiologically "he" or "she"; psychologically and socially it is neuter. It cries spontaneously for no knowledgeable reason and its hypothetical wants are experimented with until by chance one is reached and satisfied. It stops crying and sleeps. Soon it is awakened again by a discomfort—it is aware only of a generalized annoyance. The mother begins her experimentation until satisfaction is once again given. Repetition of this conditions the baby to association of the satisfactions with another being.

Partly preceding and partly following this developing identification of the mother, awarenesses, without associations or recognition, of immediate environment begin to form: light from the window or a lamp, brightness on the wall or bed, softness, hardness, sound, temperature, and on and on—increasing its world in a growing sphere. Then it discovers its toes, fingers, mouth, all explorable parts of its body—its person—its presence within that growth sphere. The mother moves in and out of the sphere. She brings comfort and satiation from those annoyances. Now a "self" is beginning to arise. A start at the "linking of the individual with his environment."[7]

Miss Kuhn's comments highlight the child's relationships with the world of nonsymbolic things, what William James referred to as the blooming, buzzing confusion of the newborn's world. In the relationship of the child to the world of nonsymbolic things (nonsymbolic from the child's viewpoint) we see communication in general at work. For the child to perceive anything—lights, shadows, or the like—communication must take place. However, for the child this is nonsymbolic communication, of essentially the same nature as that experienced by infrahuman animal organisms. Even at this stage, though, the responding others in the child's environment may indeed project a symbolic meaning on the child's nonsymbolic physical behaviors. Rene Spitz speaks to this point:

... it has become clear that at birth, and for a long time afterwards, action and communication are one. Action, performed by the neonate, is only discharge of drive. But the same action, when viewed by the observer, contains a message from the neonate.[8]

Stories of children raised by wild animals ("feral" children) and of children kept in isolation for many years also lend support to the interaction of speech communication and external stimulation in the process of linking the individual with his environment. There are over

[7] Barbara Kuhn, unpublished student essay for course in Psychology of Speech and Hearing (Communication 302, University of Wisconsin-Milwaukee), 1967.

[8] Rene A. Spitz, *No and Yes: On the Genesis of Human Communication* (New York: International Universities Press, 1957), pp. 145–46.

30 reported and partially documented cases of feral children.[9] Reports from the past 50 years are generally better documented than those from earlier times. The legend of Romulus and Remus, the brothers who founded Rome and who were supposedly suckled by a she-wolf, is shrouded in the mists of antiquity. The story of Amala and Kamala, two little girls from India who in 1921 were found living with wolves and were rescued by medical missionaries, is supported by medical histories and the narratives of those who watched over them during their lives among men. Amala, the youngest girl, died soon after being returned to civilization. Kamala lived a number of years but never developed anything near normal relationships with her surroundings. Never developing a language, Kamala never even learned such basic amenities as eating at a table.[10]

A more recent report of a feral child was distributed by *Medical World News*.[11]

Death Ends India Wolf Boy Mystery Case

From the day in 1954 that the strange child was brought in, it was difficult for the staff at Balrampur to keep from staring at him. Though severely crippled he had somehow dragged himself to a third class waiting room in a nearby Lucknow station and passed out. When found, the boy was naked and starving.

Thick calluses on his elbows and knees suggested that he had long used both to move about. X-rays of his bones indicated that he was about 11 years old when found.

The Lucknow physicians guessed that he must have been dragged off by some animal when about 1 year old.

The wolf child of Lucknow was clearly retarded and aphasic. He could howl and grunt, *but he never learned to communicate in a human way*, [italics added] not even with gestures. But his hearing and sight were not impaired. And although he had epilepsy, neurological studies never turned up any evidence of a brain lesion.

Altogether, he had lived at the hospital for 14 years, approximately the length of time that a wolf survives in captivity.

---

[9] J. A. L. Singh and Robert M. Zingg, *Wolf-Children and Feral Man* (New York: Harper & Row, Publishers, 1939).

[10] The fullest report of Amala and Kamala may be found in Singh and Zingg. A shorter description is provided in *Words and Things* by Roger Brown (New York: The Free Press, 1958), pp. 189–90.

[11] *The Milwaukee Journal*, 21 June 1968, accent section, p. 1.

Stories of children raised in isolation also lend support to the first function.[12] Cases of feral men and of children kept in isolation led Roger Brown to the conclusion that ". . . man does not develop language if he grows up among animals or in isolation. Language is acquired by the human being born into a linguistic community." [13]

The thrust of our argument thus far is that any disturbance of a human being's speech communication will have a negative effect on that individual's link with his environment. As a corollary, the environment affects the individual's speech communication; if it is other than normal, it is probable that the individual's speech communication will also deviate from normalcy. This point is made by others with slight variations. For example, M. M. Lewis states,

> The linguistic growth of a child in his social environment moves forward as the continued convergence and interaction of two groups of factors—those that spring from within the child himself and those that impinge upon him from the community around him. The growth of many other creatures has of course this dual character. Where a child's development differs is that he is so much more richly endowed with the potentialities of speech and that he grows up in a social environment permeated by symbolization, the most potent form of which is language.[14]

The self arises in communication; this is the message of George H. Mead, one of the early social psychologists. Mead and his academic descendants, known as symbolic interactionists, further state that the uniquely human self arises from communication using significant symbols—symbols which when addressed to others are at the same time addressed to oneself.

> In looking for gestures capable of becoming *significant symbols*, and so of transforming the biologic individual into a minded organism, Mead comes upon the vocal gesture. No other gesture affects the individual himself so similarly as it affects others. We hear ourselves talk as others do, but we do not see our facial expressions, nor normally watch our own actions. For Mead, the vocal gesture is the actual fountainhead of

[12] For example, see the stories of Anna and Isabelle in Brown, *op. cit.*, pp. 191–92.

[13] Brown, *op. cit.*, p. 193.

[14] *Language, Thought, and Personality: In Infancy and Childhood* (New York: Basic Books, Inc., Publishers, 1963), p. 13. A statement of a similar argument may be found in Joseph Church's *Language and the Discovery of Reality* (New York: Random House, Inc., 1961), *passim.*

language proper and all derivative forms of symbolism, and so of mind.[15]

Mead's endeavor is to show that mind and the self are without residue social emergents; and that language, in the form of the vocal gesture, provides the mechanism for their emergence.[16]

Paul F. Pfuetze speaks even more pointedly to the function of speech communication in linking the individual with his environment. "Speech communication is the chief mechanism constitutive of self-hood, language is the mark of man, . . . man is literally talked into self-hood."[17] Each human infant is a living experiment, the results of which testify to the first function of speech communication. The baby is thrust into a world which requires him to form relationships to form self. The process of relating is a communicative one. To move beyond his animal heritage and to actualize his peculiarly human attributes, the infant must relate to the world of symbols which surrounds him and which, through human interaction, will pervade his interiority. Such symbolic relating is of its nature speech communication. Only through speech communication can a child realize the beginnings of his unique humanity. Only through continued sophistication in speech communication can he fully actualize it either as an individual or as a social being. One function of speech communication is to link the human infant with his environment.

However, function one does not cease after the emergence of the child's selfhood, mind, and humanity. A mature person's ability to manipulate his inner world in a symbolic fashion is essential to his continuing self-actualization. Unless one can verbalize his convictions, assumptions, desires, goals, and drives, it is almost impossible to measure their realization or to program oneself to enhance the opportunities and possibilities of their realization. As the principle of emergent specificity operates and as the individual finds his ability to communicate particularly useful in formulating linkages outside as well as within himself, we find that he uses his speech communication to integrate himself with his immediate surroundings. In the

[15] Charles W. Morris in the introduction to George Herbert Mead's *Mind, Self and Society* (Chicago: University of Chicago Press, 1934), p. xxii.

[16] *Ibid.*, p. xiv.

[17] Paul F. Pfuetze, *Self, Society, Existence* (New York: Harper & Row, Publishers, 1961), p. 302.

early stages, this linking or integration is typified by reliance on authorities for direction and approval.[18] As the person and his communication mature, ". . . communication and cooperation with contemporaries (replaces) the former reliance upon physical and emotional assistance from elders."[19] One of the most important values of function one is helping the individual develop emotional maturity. In the process of forming communicative bonds with his culture, the individual constantly enlarges his field of contact through space and time. The self-actualizing and linking capacities of speech communication are necessary for individual maturation throughout life. In fact, when function one completely disappears and ceases operation, decrements begin rapidly to outweigh life's increments, until finally the cessation of all of an individual's speech communication does irreparable damage to his self-image and his link with his environment. "Energy bound into communication is peculiar to the life process. Perhaps it is this type of energy which controls the living organism as a whole and is dissipated in a flash at death."[20]

Obviously function one works to establish both internal and external human communicative relationships. The individual links with another individual and with many individuals, and the patterns of human communication and human relations become wider as the individual grows into society and society grows around him. The urban growth pattern throughout the world, and particularly in the United States, reflects an extension of the first function of speech communication. As Richard L. Meier states, "Cities were evolved primarily for the facilitation of human communications."[21] If they are spread over too great a land mass, people have difficulties communicating with one another. Before the advent of the mass media, if the land was too vast and communication too difficult it was awkward to form a cohesive unit or to govern adequately. This fact caused Frederick the Great to doubt the ability of the newly founded United States of America to form a stable government, since

[18] Frank E. X. Dance, "The Maturity Concept in Speech Communication," in *Adult Leadership* (December 1967), 210.

[19] Jurgen Ruesch (with Gregory Bateson), *Communication: The Matrix of Society* (New York: W. W. Norton & Company, Inc., 1951), p. 35.

[20] Halbert L. Dunn, "Communication and Purpose—Ingredients for Longevity," *Journal of Speech and Hearing Disorders*, Vol. 26, No. 2 (May 1961), 114.

[21] Richard L. Meier, *A Communications Theory of Urban Growth* (Cambridge, Mass.: The M.I.T. Press, 1962), p. 13.

the nation consisted of what seemed to be too great a land mass for people to receive a full flow of three kinds of information:

> ... first, information about the world outside; second, information from the past, with a wide range of recall and recombination; and third, information about the nation itself. Let any of these three streams be long interrupted, such as by oppression or by secrecy, and the society becomes an automaton, a walking corpse. It loses control over its own behavior, not only for some of its parts, but also eventually at its very top.[22]

Fortunately for our nation, the instruments of mass communication have helped us reduce the staggering problems of human communication over great distances in short time spans.

In speech communication human relations exist and society inheres. The first function of speech communication is to link an individual with his environment.

5.3.2. Function 2: The development of higher mental processes. The progression from (a) the infant's initial perception, apprehension, and production of stimuli to (b) his production of vocalizations or of "speech" to (c) the linking of genetically determined speech to culturally determined "language" resulting in the acquisition of external "speech communication" to (d) the gradual internalization of speech communication mirrors the development of higher mental processes.[23]

The events listed above are presented in what is conceived to be both their chronological and hierarchial order. Certainly they are presented in order of increasing specificity of individual response, starting with rather generalized behavior and becoming progressively more refined. Such a progression exemplifies the process that has been called the principle of emergent specificity. This principle suggests that throughout the course of individual human development we may perceive a movement from the general to the specific,

[22] Karl W. Deutsch, *The Nerves of Government* (New York: The Free Press, 1963), p. 129.

[23] L. S. Vygotsky, *Thought and Language* (New York: John Wiley & Sons, Inc., 1962), *passim*. F. E. X. Dance, "Toward a Theory of Human Communication," in *Human Communication Theory*, F. E. X. Dance, ed. (New York: Holt, Rinehart and Winston, Inc., 1967), pp. 288–309. Also Werner and Kaplan, *Symbol Formation* (New York: John Wiley & Sons, Inc., 1963).

from the undifferentiated to the differentiated. From the moment of conception the emerging human (embryo, fetus, infant, child, adolescent, adult) is involved in a continuing reciprocal relationship with the environment. This relationship produces increasingly finer, more differentiated responses to the environment by the individual. Speech communication, once it has developed, plays a principal role in the sequence.

The human organism is the obvious material prerequisite for any learning or maturation. Patterns of maturation and capacities for learning are built into the individual from the beginning, even though the manner in which and extent to which individual patterns and capacities are actualized depends on the environment. Patterns and capacities for which the basic organism is unequipped cannot be actualized, just as a machine requiring the simultaneous application of four hands for operation cannot be manipulated by a single individual without human or mechanical assistance.

A baby must be able to perceive internal and external happenings or stimuli before he can either select those to which he gives special attention (apprehension) or have certain stimulus patterns forced on him by the physical or social environment. If there is internal deprivation, such as that which results from brain damage, there will be deprivation on the level of organic perception/apprehension; consequently there will be inevitable disorganization of experiences and behaviors dependent on this basic level for their initiation, development, and continuing support.

Soon after the infant's initial development of perceptual capacities, and usually simultaneously with birth, begins the process of vocalization.[24] It is the refinement of this process, the production of phonated and articulated sound, which we call speech. Speech, thus defined and presuming adequate physiological and neurological bases, limits itself to vocal, sound-making behavior. In acquiring speech ability the child passes through certain fairly well defined stages of development. The developmental process begins with the undifferentiated birth cry and progresses through increasingly refined approximations of the sound system reflected in the vocal behavior of the responding others in the child's environment. Speech is a genetically determined activity. The capacity and the neurological

---

[24] Dorothea McCarthy in *Manual of Child Psychology* (2nd. ed.), Leonard Carmichael, ed. (New York: John Wiley & Sons, Inc., 1954), pp. 492–630, *passim.*

"wiring" for vocal sound making are built into the organism, part of the genetic code and heritage of the human child. Normal infants do not need to be taught to make vocal noises, but do so naturally and spontaneously.

When a child's "speech" begins to interact with the language of his culture a qualitatively new process begins: that of speech communication, or spoken symbolic interaction. The acquisition of speech and the acquisition of speech communication (that process wherein genetically determined speech and culturally determined language begin to interact) follow similar but not identical paths. Speech communication heralds the use of speech for significance, abstraction, and thought. As Vygotsky states, "In the phylogeny of thought and speech, a prelinguistic phase in the development of thought and a preintellectual phase in the development of speech are clearly discernible."[25] We shall first present some of the findings concerning the speech development of a child, and then those concerning his language development.

Not enough empirical or experimental evidence has been gathered to allow the construction of a chart detailing stages in the child's formulation or acquisition of speech communication. The evidence we now have indicates that the lines of precognitive speech acquisition and prelinguistic cognitive development seem to intersect around the child's twenty-fourth month of life. At that point speech and language merge, never again to be totally separated, to initiate speech communication and to bring the child to the point of engaging in spoken symbolic interaction. All of the stages in the child's acquisition of speech/language contribute substantively to his formulation of speech communication. Many variables, not accounted for on the speech/language acquisition charts, also influence the child's preparation for and actualization of speech communication. For example, the child develops intrapersonal communication skills which seem to be independent of speech, skills wherein action, the expression of drive, and communication are one and the same for the infant although they may be meaningfully interpreted as distinct messages by the responding other. A child's kicking may not be meant by the kicker to communicate anything but may be perceived by the responding adult as a reaction against binding blankets, and thus may communicate to the adult the child's desire for a

[25] Vygotsky, *op. cit.*, p. 41.

SOME STAGES IN THE CHILD'S ACQUISITION OF SPEECH
(The stages overlap)

Genetic: Girls develop language competence faster than boys.

Age in months		Speech behavior	
Birth	Crying	Undifferentiated crying; a total response to life. Within a week the child begins to show the results of external environmental response and reinforcement resulting in the beginning of differentiation according to the source of discomfort. Cooing and gurgling sounds predominate.	
3	Babbling	Mainly unlearned play-experimentation with the body's sound-making equipment. Both vowels and consonants are produced.	
4		This stage appears in both the hearing and the nonhearing child. The babbling stage enhances the child's flexible use of his	
5		sound-making capacities.	
6	Lalling	The infant's imitation of his own sound-making, for pleasure and practice.	One of the first points of difference between hearing and nonhearing children. The nonhearing child does not progress through either lalling or echolalia.
8	Echolalia	The infant's imitation of the sound-making of others, for play and prac-	
10		tice and also for the reinforcement often bestowed on the child by those being imitated.	
12		Continued practice in approximating the vocal sound-making of responding others. Differentiation and refinement of vocal sound-making insure that the normal child by six or seven years of age has acquired almost adult proficiency	
72		in the comprehension and production of the culturally appropriate articulatory and phonemic repertoire.	

readjustment of the bedclothes. In this example we note both intrapersonal and interpersonal communication—both at this time independent of speech/language on the part of the child. He is developing a bodily repertoire for the communication of information. Such nonverbal communication will prove useful throughout his life.

The child's total environment also contributes to his future speech communication. In many ways, the quality of his early communication environment is the most important external factor influencing his acquisition of communication skills and development of communication competencies. Research indicates that only

SOME STAGES IN THE CHILD'S ACQUISITION OF LANGUAGE
(The stages overlap)

Age in months	Language behavior
8 10	Beginning of language comprehension. Language comprehension has priority over language production and ordinarily precedes it by a few months.
12	The appearance of the first word, usually a noun.
18	The child has acquired between 20 and 100 words, generally nouns and some verbs; he produces single-word sentences; and his production is about 25% intelligible to responding others.
24	The child has acquired between 200 and 300 words, mostly nouns and verbs; he produces two-word sentences; and his production is about 66% intelligible to responding others.
36	About 900 words including nouns, verbs, pronouns, and adjectives are used to produce three-word sentences which are 90% intelligible to responding others.
48	About 1,500 words including all parts of speech.
60	The child's language production reaches 100% intelligibility for responding others.
72 84	The average child has mastered practically all the syntactical forms and constructions of his language.

children develop communication skills and competencies faster than children with siblings, that children with siblings develop communication skills and competencies faster than twins, and that all children born into a normal family develop communication skills and compentencies faster than children born into and raised within institutions. Environmental deprivation can affect the child's speech/language/communication development negatively as surely as can brain damage or other internal deprivations.

Through the varieties of his environment, the child is also exposed to events requiring peer-group communication as well as communication with responding adults. These situations help develop expectations which will continue to play an important role in the individual's communication throughout his life. The infant, and later the child, begins to shape his relationship with authority as well as to shape his own self-image through his communication environment.

At the intersection of the child's speech acquisition and his language acquisition occurs the initiation of a new form of behavior, the child's speech communication. "... [T]he most important discovery is that at a certain moment at about age two the curves of development of thought and speech, till then separate, meet and join to initiate a new form of behavior. . . . This crucial instant, . . . speech begins to serve intellect, and thoughts begin to be spoken. . . ."[26] We do not mean to assert that thought and language are one and the same; certainly there are aspects of cognitive functioning which are other than aspects of linguistic behavior. However, in this instance the thought to which Vygotsky seems to be alluding is characterized by the beginnings of higher mental processes which always seem to be manifested in language.

When genetically determined speech is linked to the system of symbols—language—which is transmitted to the child by his culture, we witness the creation of a new level of behavior, the level of speech communication. The child moves from meaningless vocalizations and random production of syllables to the joining of syllables for the purpose of sharing and conveying symbols—from "gaga" to "mama."

At this point the impact of a language on the development of thought becomes of special interest. Philosopher Ludwig Wittgenstein stated, "What can be said at all can be said clearly, and whereof one cannot speak thereof one must be silent."[27] This position was made even more important by the point of view of the anthropologist Edward Sapir, whose thoughts were expanded by another anthropologist, Benjamin Lee Whorf:

> The central idea of the Sapir-Whorf hypothesis is that language functions, not simply as a device for reporting experience, but also, and more significantly, as a way of defining experience for its speakers. . . .
>
> It is evident (if this statement is valid) that language plays a large and significant role in the totality of culture. Far from being simply a technique of communication, it is itself a way of directing the perceptions of its speakers and it provides for them habitual modes of analyzing experience into significant categories. And to the extent that languages differ markedly from each other, so should we expect to find significant and formidable barriers to cross-cultural communication and understanding.[28]

[26] *Ibid.*, p. 43.

[27] Ludwig Wittgenstein, *Tractatus Logico-Philosophicus*, trans. D. F. Pears and B. F. McGuinness (London: Routledge and Kegan Paul, New York: Humanities Press, 1961).

[28] Harry Hoijer, "The Sapir-Whorf Hypothesis," in *Language in Culture*, H. Hoijer, ed. (Chicago: University of Chicago Press, 1954), pp. 93–94.

The Sapir-Whorf hypothesis, also known as "linguistic determinism" or "linguistic relativity," is difficult to deal with since an individual's native language is learned so early and holistically that its effect on the individual is almost necessarily outside the individual's conscious, critical capacity. That language has an effect on thought is patent and not open to serious question; what is questionable is the extent of its influence. Considerations vary. George Orwell, in his novel *1984*, suggests that by inculcating the inhabitants of the Orwellian future with the language called "Newspeak" the state will make those inhabitants totally unable to think of things inimical to itself, since "Newspeak" contains neither the semantic nor the syntactical wherewithal to support such treasonous thoughts. Others believe that the influence of language on thought is so insignificant as to be negligible.

Language *does* affect thought. That position is consonant with the effect of the child's total environment, of which his language is an important part, on his growth and development. A linguistically deprived child may well be socially deprived—such is the finding of researchers interested in the effect of institutionalization or economic poverty on children.[29] However, differences in language do not result in total differences in thought processes or patterns, since such processes and patterns are also related to levels of existential reality subserving the cultural language—levels such as neurophysiological functioning, perceptual adequacy, and similarity of external physical stimuli across cultures and language boundaries. In Pavlovian terms, the second signal system is always rooted in, and affected by, the organism's subcortical and first cortical signal system. The student of speech communication must always be alert to the effect of language on thought and perception without consciously or unconsciously ascribing to language the role of master of thought.

In its beginning stage speech communication is external; the child says aloud "papa" or "mama." As the child matures and develops, external speech communication is gradually internalized. The child says "mama" aloud and at the same time says "mama" to himself. This interior representation of "mama" elevates the child's capacity

[29] Basil Bernstein, "Elaborated and Restricted Codes: Their Social Origins and Some Consequences," in "The Ethnography of Communication," *American Anthropologist Special Publications*, J. J. Gumperz and Dell Hymes, eds., Vol. 66, No. 2 (1964), 55–69.

for abstraction and for flexibility in adaptation and control of himself and his environment. Around his fifth year the child's external speech communication begins to become sufficiently internalized so that he is increasingly capable of solving complex problems without the aid of vocalization. This stage of inner speech marks the completion of the formative stages of speech communication in the child. Henceforth the chore becomes one not of development but of refinement and sophistication.

In the final stage the child gains a hitherto unavailable control of his own internal and external behavior as well as of the behavior of others. Of course he does not at first realize this power, but such realization generally comes quickly as he tries through his external and internal speech communication to exert more and more influence over his environment. The child's ability to represent his external reality internally through speech communication allows him to manipulate fantasy and to engage in higher mental processes in the absence of the specific external stimuli which match his internal thoughts.

> Silent thinking, though we believe it to be a succession of pictures, is really conducted largely in unspoken words. Some dream analyses uncover the most astounding verbal material even on the primitive level of ideation. No one knows how words which are certainly not articulated—sometimes, indeed, are illustrated in a way that hides their effective presence from the thinker or dreamer himself—enter into cerebral processes; no one knows how far the various language functions permeate our mental life, but with every new research the soundings go deeper.[30]

Inner speech is not the same as silent speech; it is not an extension of whispering. In whispering, speech communication is simply reduced in audibility but maintains all the semantic and syntactical qualities of external speech communication. Inner speech communication is markedly different from external speech communication in terms of audience orientation, semantic load, and syntactical structure. Luria speaks to all of these differences when he says,

---

[30] Susanne K. Langer, *Mind: An Essay on Human Feeling*, Vol. 1 (Baltimore: The Johns Hopkins Press, 1967), p. 60.

Because it is "speech for oneself," serving above all to fix and regulate intellectual processes, and because it has a largely predictive character, inner speech necessarily ceases to be detailed and grammatical. It contracts, acquires a folded, grammatical structure, always preserving, however, the possibility of developing into a complete, differentiated and complex utterance.[31]

Vygotsky, in *Thought and Language*, detailed three specific characteristics which distinguish inner speech from external speech. [32] These three characteristics of inner speech communication are well suited for the chores of thinking and planning. Inner speech communication is characterized by silence, condensation, and synthesized meaning. Silence is self-explanatory. Condensation refers to a high degree of ellipsis and syntactic incompleteness. Synthesized meaning denotes that in inner speech communication a single word often carries meanings garnered from diverse experiences and settings, so that that particular word carries many more meanings, overtones, and allusions for the individual than he could successfully communicate to another simply through the use of the same single word. In translating an idea from inner speech communication to external speech communication one must engage in substantial semantic and syntactic development.

Some of the research evidence concerning the second function of speech communication comes from the work of Soviet scholars. The Soviet work, which is valuable although it often uses methods different from those used in much non-Soviet research, has developed from the insights of scholars such as Sechenov and Pavlov. In 1866 Ivan Mikhailovich Sechenov, father of Russian physiology, published his essay "Reflexes of the Brain," in which he generalized from his experiments with frogs to the concept that all mental processes of man are reflex in nature.[33] In 1902 Ivan Petrovich Pavlov set out to examine the working of the higher nervous processes or cerebral mechanisms in man, using the technique of the conditional reflex which had first been described by the French

---

[31] A. R. Luria, "Speech Development and the Formation of Mental Processes," in *Handbook of Contemporary Soviet Psychology*, Michael Cole and Irving Maltzman, eds. (New York: Basic Books, Inc., Publishers, 1969), pp. 121–62.

[32] *Ibid.*, pp. 146–48.

[33] I. M. Sechenov, *Reflexes of The Brain*, trans. S. Belsky (Cambridge, Mass.: The M.I.T. Press, 1965).

philosopher René Descartes. By the end of Pavlov's career, in 1936, he had broadly sketched a schema meant to describe how man thinks and reasons: the schema of the *three signal systems*. In his early research and writing, Pavlov emphasized that all animate matter exhibited certain inborn, innate, or subcortical activities—activities reflexive in nature in that they were necessary reactions to strictly defined stimuli under strictly defined conditions. An example of such a subcortical reflex is the coughing reflex that clears the throat of intruding objects. A similar reflex, also subcortical, is the gag reflex that occurs when a solid object is thrust far back in the mouth. Both of these reflexes take place without the need for any mental information processing on the part of the individual. Subcortical reflexes do not depend on cerebral sophistication either for their existence or for their continuation. They are often carried out on a simple spinal level. This sytem, then, can be referred to as the *subcortical signal system* (SCSS).

With the addition of elaborated cerebral–neurological structures in higher-level animals, Pavlov found that the organism responded also to a system which depends on cortical structures for their elaboration. These cortical signals alert the animal to environmental stimuli through distance receptors such as sight and hearing. This sytem Pavlov referred to as the *first* (cortical) *signal system* (ISS).

Considerably later in his research activities, Pavlov concluded that man alone is capable of linking multiple stimuli together by a unitary verbal signal. This unique human capacity Pavlov called the *second signal system* (IISS). The IISS depends on the presence of a cortex.

In schematic form, then, the Pavlovian conception of man's higher intellectual processes is composed of one subcortical signal system, one cortical signal system, and a second cortical signal system which equates with what we have been calling speech communication.

II cortical signal system (speech communication)
I cortical signal system

cortex —————————————————————————— cortex

subcortical signal system

Here is how Pavlov describes these systems:

SCSS   The reflex of self-defense. The strong carnivorous animal preys on weaker animals which, if they waited to defend themselves until the teeth of the foe were in their flesh, would speedily be exterminated.[34]

ISS   The case takes on a different aspect when the defense reflex is called into play by the sights and sounds of the enemy's approach. Then the prey has a chance to save itself by hiding or flight.[35]

IISS   In man, however ... the most valuable signaling medium ... (is) speech.[36] Speech, because of the entire preceding life of the adult, is connected with all the internal and external stimuli which can reach the cortex, signaling all of them and replacing all of them, and therefore it can call forth all those reactions of the organism which are normally determined by the actual stimuli themselves.[37]

In the Pavlovian examples given, the organism solely dependent on the subcortical signal system must wait for the direct attack of the predator before its self-defense reflex is called into play. For example, if a decorticated rabbit were attacked by a weasel, the rabbit would sit quietly in the presence of the approaching weasel and would not try to escape until the teeth of the weasel had actually sunk into its flesh. However, when in addition to the subcortical signal system the first (cortical) signal system is present, and a corticated rabbit is faced with an approaching weasel, the rabbit, through his distance receptors of sight, hearing, and smell, responds defensively to the signs of the approaching weasel before the weasel has a chance to grab the rabbit. In the third example, man, with the tremendous advantage of his second signal system (or

[34] I. P. Pavlov, *Conditioned Reflexes: An Investigation of the Physiological Activity of the Cerebral Cortex*, trans. G. V. Anrep, ed. (New York: Dover Publications, Inc., 1960), p. 14.

[35] *Ibid.*, p. 14.

[36] It is evident from the internal usage and other allusions to the same subject that Pavlov when using the word *speech* is referring to the same behavioral manifestations that we have called "speech communication."

[37] Pavlov, *Conditioned Reflexes*, pp. 406–7.

speech communication), can respond to signs of signs, or *symbols*, of approaching danger, and the symbols can elicit all those reflex mechanisms of flight or fight which in other systems depend on the actual presence of the concrete stimulus.

The IISS is, in Pavlov's view, the determining characteristic of man's higher nervous activity. Speech communication, in the Pavlovian conception, has made us human, yet speech communication, the IISS, is governed by the same laws that govern the subcortical signal system and the first signal system, since all of these signal systems are dependent on the activity of the same nervous tissue.[38]

The IISS provides man with a signal of signals. Man's speech communication allows him to use a single symbol to represent many sensory signals. Symboling is the essence of the process of abstraction and generalization central to studies of concept formation and of the relationship of thought and speech communication.

It is difficult to find subjects ideally suited for examination of the role of speech communication in the development of mental processes. Professor Luria and a colleague, F. I. Yudovich, found appropriate subjects in the persons of five-year-old identical twins. In the words of the researchers,

> The twins suffered from a peculiar defect which created conditions for a retardation of speech development; added to this was the "twin situation" which did not create an objective necessity for developing language and so constituted a factor which fixed this retardation.
>
> ... [T]he twins were unable to detach the word from action, to master orienting, planning activity, to formulate the aims of activity with the aid of speech and so to subordinate their further activity to this verbal formulation. Therefore, even at the age of five to five and a half years, our twins could not master skills nor organize complex play of a kind proper to children of this age, and were unable to engage in productive, meaningful activity. Their intellectual operations thus remained very limited; even such operations as elementary classification were beyond them.
>
> In order to discover the factors that played a leading role in the development of speech and the changes that might be brought about in the construction of the twins' mental life as a result of the rapid acquisition of language, we undertook a special experiment.

---

[38] For example, laws essential to the neuronal structure itself, such as the law of strength of stimulus, the law of neuronal fatigue, or the law of neuronal summation.

It was necessary, to ensure a rapid development of speech, to create an objective necessity for using language in the company of speaking children. We, therefore, removed the "twin situation" by separating the children and placing them in separate, parallel groups in a kindergarten and then observed the changes that took place in their speech. Subsequently, we conducted a special systematic experiment in teaching speech with one of the twins, with the aim of developing perception of speech, the habit of making use of developed sentences, etc.

Our experiment produced very rapid results.

As a result of removal of the "twin situation" primitive speech, interlocked with practical activity, very quickly fell into the background and in the new situation the children were soon in a position to pass on to communicating with the aid of a normal language system.

Three months after the experiment began we could already observe substantial improvements in the twins' speech. Leaving aside small phonetic defects, the lexicology and grammar of their speech approximated to the normal speech of their counterparts. Their speech also fulfilled new functions which had formerly been absent; in place of speech interlocked with direct activity, or expressive speech, there developed narrative and then planning speech.

Even more significant was the fact that the whole structure of the mental life of both twins was simultaneously and sharply changed. Once they acquired an objective language system, the children were able to formulate the aims of their activity verbally and after only three months we observed the beginnings of meaningful play; there arose the possibility of productive, constructive activity in the light of formulated aims, and to an important degree there were separated out a series of intellectual operations which shortly before this were only in an embryonic state.

In the course of further observations we were able to note cardinal improvements in the structure of the twins' mental life which we could only attribute to the influence of the one changed factor—the acquisition of a language system.[39]

5.3.3. Function 3: The regulation of behavior. One of the functions of speech communication is the regulation of behavior. When speech communication is taking place, behavior is being regulated: either the behavior of others or of oneself. Using the concept of the significant symbol, speech communication may be functioning at one and the same time to regulate the behavior of self and of others.

[39] A. R. Luria and F. I. Yudovich, *Speech and the Development of Mental Processes in the Child*, trans. J. Simon (London: Staples Press, 1959), pp. 120–23.

That we use speech communication to get others to do our bidding is obvious. "Come here," "give me the pencil," "stop that noise." With each of these instructions we have tried to regulate the behavior of someone through speech communication. Persuasion, propaganda, and attitude change are all concerned with the regulation of behavior through speech communication. Our success in changing the external behavior of others indicates success in changing or regulating their internal behavior. Symbolic suggestion, when manifested in threats, voodoo rites, and promises for the future, seems to be able to produce alterations of internal processes in others.

Advertising, education, and propaganda all testify to the role of speech communication in the regulation of human behavior. Through mass media and face-to-face speech communication the commercial advertiser tries to change the attitudes of the buying public toward a given product. The political propagandist, again through mass media and face-to-face speech communication, tries to change the attitudes, opinions, and beliefs of his audience toward a political figure, belief system, or party. The educator, mostly through speech communication, tries to assist his pupil in the process of self-development and actualization of potentialities. Books such as *To Change a Nation* [40] and *Thought Reform and the Psychology of Totalism*[41] document specific instances and campaigns in which speech communication has been used to regulate the behavior of individuals and of nations.

We also use speech communication to regulate our own behavior. Such regulation may be the result of vocalized, silent, or inner speech communication. Suppose you were working outdoors, sawing a board, when you realized that your thumb was directly in line with the saw blade. At that moment you may well have given yourself an order such as, "Dummy, get your thumb out of the way." This order is spoken aloud, and you quickly match your motor behavior to your verbal regulation. Adults often regulate their complex self-behaviors through silent speech communication. Driving through an unfamiliar city you stop to ask directions, they are given, you rehearse them silently to yourself, and then you start to follow them. While traversing the route you are constantly silently giving yourself directions such as "Turn right at the third stoplight and then go east

[40] Franklin W. Houn, *To Change a Nation* (New York: The Free Press, 1961).
[41] Robert Jay Lifton, *Thought Reform and the Psychology of Totalism* (New York: W. W. Norton & Company, Inc., 1961).

for two blocks." This is an example of the regulation of external behavior of self through silent speech communication. We also use speech communication to regulate our internal behavior. We use speech communication to make our hearts beat faster, to create internal states of self-satisfaction or self-criticism, to make ourselves feel guilty or justified, to create courage and sometimes foolhardy self-confidence.

Speech communication functions to regulate behavior. Depending on the communicative event, this regulation may be one or a combination of internal or external, of the self or of others.

The traffic route example also dramatizes an important distinction between silent speech communication and inner speech communication. In the example, although you speak silently to yourself, the directions are usually semantically and syntactically expanded. As a result, even though the directions are given silently, were it possible to pick up and amplify the minute electrical potentials from your articulatory and phonatory muscles and to convert them into audible sound, that amplified sound would probably be recognizable and meaningful to another listener. On the other hand, even when you are driving through a familiar city you may be giving self-direction through true inner speech communication. These directions would exhibit the characteristics of inner speech communication—not only silence, but ellipsis and semantic and syntactic compression. Were such inner speech communication made audible, the resultant sound would most likely be unintelligible to external listeners.

In most interpersonal situations, the interchange of speech communication helps both participants make adjustments throughout the event. The first speaker's "hello" creates a situation in which the second speaker's response repertoire is normally structured by situational expectations. The response to the "hello" is the product of the first speaker's behavior as well as of the respondent's intent. As the dialogue progresses, each participant shares in shaping the expectations and choices of the other through speech communication. In this instance, speech communication regulates, at one and the same time, each speaker's self-behavior as well as the behavior of the responding other.

The regulation of behavior through speech communication commences from the outside in, then is internalized to provide self-regulation, and finally is consciously expanded as an instrument to control others.

When a mother says to her child, "That is a cup," the child turns his head and looks at the named object. When mother says to him, "Clap!", he raises his hands and claps. The mother's remark regulates the child's behavior.

However, the ability to regulate another's behavior with the help of speech is only one aspect of this important function of speech. When a child subordinates himself to a verbal order of an adult, he assimilates this method of organizing actions. He himself begins to form the pattern of his own future actions. Speech reflects the connections and relationships of reality and formulates the modes of future action. Speech, addressed as an order to oneself, quickly becomes one of the most important methods of regulating behavior in the development of the child.

Speech revives traces of past experience, the signals of which are those real signals which, like all others, are only signals but are incomparably more generalized and labile. The direction of his behavior with the help of these signals is what basically distinguishes the mental activity of man from the behavior of animals.[42]

All this justifies a deduction of great significance for future investigations. To begin with, the child's speech, by replacing a directly perceptible stimulus and direct reinforcement, serves as a means of obtaining a fuller reflection of reality; but, as its develops, it increasingly becomes a means of systematizing past experience, and so a means whereby the child orientates himself in the directly perceived real world, and regulates his actions.[43]

As noted earlier, the infant is tremendously affected by his environment and by his adult models. The adults with whom he interacts play a dominant role in the shaping of his personality and self-image. Through his adult models the infant comes into contact with the world of responding others and develops his expectations for all responding others. The adult, through his speech communication, shapes and regulates the behavior of the infant and in doing so provides the infant with a model for self-development and self-regulation. With the advent of the infant's speech communication, he practices regulating his behavior through speech communication and then expands his efforts to regulate the behavior of responding others.

[42] A. R. Luria, *The Mentally Retarded Child* (Oxford: Pergamon Press, 1963), p. 7.
[43] A. R. Luria, "The Role of Language in the Formation of Temporary Connections," in *Psychology in the Soviet Union*, B. Simon, ed. (Stanford, Calif.: Stanford University Press, 1957), p. 117.

In the early stages the child becomes conscious only that there is communication. Then he becomes conscious that the primary medium for communication is speech communication, the wedding of speech and language. Finally, the child discovers that speech communication is not only the means by which he can exchange information with others, but is also the means by which he can himself examine and order reality for purposes of analysis and application. Speech communication brings order out of disorder and extends the power of the child, as well as of all men, over his environment. As Jerome Bruner says when commenting on the role played by language in the learning process, "Teaching is vastly facilitated by the medium of language, which ends by not only being the medium used for exchange but the instrument that the learner can then use himself in bringing order into the environment." [44] Speech communication transmits information and also holds information together in the experience of the perceiver. Communication is at the core of organization, and all organization, either in general or in specific embodiments, is an example of communicative interaction.

5.4. Functional Ceilings. The degree to which an individual realizes or actualizes the three functions of speech communication depends on both his basic human physiological/psychological equipment and the manner in which he uses this equipment within his environment. The primary acquisition of speech communication *qua* speech communication is species specific. All human beings, all members of the species *Homo sapiens*, will in the course of their natural development acquire speech communication. Such acquisition is not an artifact of education or of developmental sophistication, but is rather the simple result of being born "human" with the physiological/psychological equipment such birth implies. The old belief that speech is an overlaid function—that the organs man uses in speaking all have other, more basic, uses on which the act of speaking is overlaid—is challenged by the position that man has by his very nature an organ or organs (for example, the cerebral cortex) which is essentially information-processing. Speech communication indeed makes use of bodily organs and organ complexes which perform behaviors other than speaking. However, there may be in man organs

---

[44] Jerome Bruner, *Toward a Theory of Instruction* (Cambridge, Mass.: Harvard University Press, 1966), p. 6.

or organ complexes which, although morphologically similar to those in other animals, behave differently than in other animals and have as a peculiar function the production of speech communication. If that is the case, then man's capacity to acquire speech communication is a species capacity, and individual difference lies not in the acquisition but in the performance. How an individual uses the species-specific capacity for speech communication depends on individual talents and the individual's environment—or on the traditional combination of nature and nurture. Although the individual's human physiology sets the ceilings for his functional development, such development depends on the experiences to which the individual is exposed and exposes himself.

5.4.1. **Functional decrements and increments.**   Insofar as an individual, either congenitally or through trauma, exhibits decrements in his speech communication, to a similar degree he will exhibit decrements in the functions of speech communication. Insofar as an individual is successful in enhancing his speech communication development, to a similar degree the functions of speech communication in that individual will be enhanced.

5.4.2. **Functional emergence.** Although it is impossible at this time to state the exact chronological order of emergence of the functions of speech communication in an individual, it seems likely that they emerge in the order presented in this chapter: first, the linking of the individual with his environment; second, the development of higher mental processes; and third, the regulation of behavior. The first function need not be fully developed before the second function begins to emerge, nor need the second be fully developed before the third begins to emerge. All three functions are, in essence, immanent in the human being.

5.4.3. **Functional interrelationships.** In the process of their emergence the functions are additive; that is, once the first function has emerged it enhances the development of the second function, and the first and second enhance the development of the third. When the three functions have all emerged to a certain, at this time unknown, extent they become inextricably interwoven, and separating them for purposes of examination and discussion becomes an entirely academic effort.

5.5. Functional Projection. We know that individuals often project their feelings onto others. The threatened person feels that responding others are threatening, the fearful person sees others as people to be feared, the friendly person finds it easy to be so since he sees other people as friendly, the deceitful individual distrusts others since he tends to project his nature and intent upon them. Given the functions of speech communication described in this chapter, it seems reasonable to postulate that human beings project their internalized speech communication functions onto their externalized interpersonal social structures and organizations. Social problems often have counterparts in familial and interpersonal breakdowns. The international and intersocietal conflicts that unfortunately typify our world can be viewed as magnifications of the tensions that all too often permeate interpersonal relationships between employer and employee, husband and wife, parent and child, those in authority and those under authority. These interpersonal stresses can often be traced to intrapersonal disruptions in the individual's capacity to relate to his environment or to regulate his own behavior. All too frequently intrapersonal disruptions and interpersonal conflicts are manifested in suicides, mental illness, ulcers, nervousness, bickering, hostility, murder, vindictiveness, aimless striking out at others, destructive behaviors, and the artificial solutions offered through LSD, tranquilizers, and narcotics. Our social problems are often magnifications of our personal problems. The very personal conflicts of Herod and Hitler both worked havoc on the world around them. Speech communication functions are originally projected in the familial primary group. The family, in turn, is the organizational prototype which prepares (or fails to prepare) the individual for organizational roles in the larger society, so that eventually we see reflected in society as a whole the functions (whether adaptive or maladaptive) of speech communication in the individual.

If the stated functions are accurate, then the levels of communication research, whether it concerns the cell, the individual, the family, organizations, nations, cultures, or societies, are all related to the manner in which speech communication links the individual with his society, assists him in the development of his higher mental processes, and helps him regulate his behavior and the behavior of his fellows.

SUMMARY

1. Speech communication functions so importantly in the life of a human being that an understanding of speech communication is at the very core of a liberal education.

2. "Function" as used in this chapter describes a relationship wherein one quality is so related to another quality that it depends on and varies with it. In addition, function is independent of intent.

3. "Purpose" is distinguished from function by virtue of being the product of intent, either unconscious or conscious.

4. Speech communication has three functions: (1) the linking of the individual with his environment, (2) the development of higher mental processes, and (3) the regulation of behavior.

5. A mature person's ability to manipulate his inner world in a symbolic fashion is essential to his continuing self-actualization.

6. It is in speech communication that human relations exist and society inheres.

7. The progression from the infant's (a) initial perception, apprehension, and production of stimuli, to (b) his production of vocalizations or of "speech," to (c) the linking of genetically determined "speech" to culturally determined "language" resulting in the acquisition of external speech communication, to (d) the gradual internalization of speech communication mirrors the development of higher mental processes.

8. Inner speech communication is characterized by silence, condensation, and synthesized meaning.

9. Speech communication may be functioning at one and the same time to regulate the behavior of self and of others.

10. Although the individual's human physiology sets the ceiling for his functional development, such development depends on the experiences to which the individual is exposed and exposes himself.

11. The three functions, when they have emerged, are dynamically interrelated.

12. Human beings project their internalized speech communication functions onto their externalized interpersonal social structures and organizations.

EXERCISES

1. In small discussion groups identify and list not more than three or four questions you would ask of four- or five-year-old children to determine the role of overt speech communication in their behavior. (For example, What parts of your body do you use when you think?) Ask your questions of three children in the appropriate age group. In the same small discussion groups compare the results of your observations.

2. Drawing from your experience, give an example of the use of speech communication in the regulation of behavior (for example, a personal case of successful/unsuccessful persuasion).

3. After interviewing faculty members in sociology, psychology, or other related disciplines, prepare a researched speech concerning one of the three functions of speech communication in the mentally ill.

ADDITIONAL READINGS

The materials cited in the footnotes constitute sufficient additional readings for this chapter.

Chapter 6

THE

MODES

OF

SPEECH

COMMUNICATION

Conceptual Term: **MODE** (Modality)

Conceptual Description. *The method through which one manifests speech communication. The individual operational system for the conveyance of speech communication. The means of acting or doing. The modes of speech communication are auditory, kinesthetic/ proprioceptive, olfactory, tactile, and visual.*[1]

Discussion. *Modes are integral to the human communicator; that is, a mode is determined by the capabilities of the individual human being.*[2] *Modes, being tied to the human organism, are not exactly the same as channels. There is a complementary relationship between sender modes and receiver modes.*

Examples. *Speech communication is primarily trans-*

[1] In a purely speculative vein, it could be supposed that the early (both phylo-genetic and ontogenetic) modal hierarchy for speech communication would be (1) auditory, (2) kinesthetic/proprioceptive, (3) visual, (4) tactile, and (5) olfactory. However, it might well be true that this modal hierarchical order alters during the course of development of speech communication in the individual.

[2] "The very construction of the human organism thus provides a variety of modalities for the registration of excitation, and for its processing and regulation." Sibylle K. Escalona, *The Roots of Individuality* (Chicago: Aldine-Atherton, Inc., 1968), p. 35.

mitted through sound. It is coded by the sender into vocal stimuli and is complementarily analyzed by the receiver through audition. Thus one of the modes of speech communication is the auditory mode. The auditory mode may be supplemented or augmented by the visual mode through accompanying gestures. Whereas a telephone wire may serve as a speech communication channel, it is not a mode or modality of speech communication. Prior to being analyzed by a human receiver the electrical impulses must be transformed once again into stimuli appropriate to a human modal analyzer such as the ear or the eye.

Since modes have differing physiological and psychological characteristics, it is helpful to understand their distinctions. (In actual usage, most of us handle modal choice on an automatic and unconscious level. At times, however, it may be to our advantage to have our modal choices under greater voluntary control.)

6.1. Table 6.1 presents primary analyzers. The primary analyzers for one mode may well serve as secondary analyzers for another mode. For example, in the overall process of "tasting" a wine, the gustatory modality works closely with the olfactory modality, and both may be affected by the visual modality. You can also demonstrate the interaction of visual, olfactory, and gustatory modalities by using food colors to alter the regular appearance of table foods. How about a bite of black mashed potatoes? You can sometimes affect the way in which a person perceives the taste of something simply by suggesting to the person, prior to tasting, that the substance *looks* spoiled. Thus, the modes overlap.

A speaker who says, "A terrible thing has happened in our society" while smiling broadly is communicating two different things and challenging the receiver to discover a way of reconciling the discordant messages presented by the acoustic and visual modes.

6.2. Although the auditory modality penetrates to the very depths of personhood, its importance does not rely solely on metaphysical or philosophical grounds. The importance of the auditory modality is rooted in basic neurophysiology. Through the auditory modality the greatest proportion of speech communication is perceived and

TABLE 6.1.   MODES, STIMULI, AND PRIMARY ANALYZERS[3]

Stimulus	Mode	Primary analyzer[4]
Sound waves	Auditory	The ear and associated neuronal pathways and cortical areas
Light	Visual	The eye and associated neuronal pathways and cortical areas
Pressure	Tactile[5] Proprioceptive Kinesthetic	The skin, internal organs, the musculature, the nervous system, and associated neuronal pathways and cortical areas
Odors	Olfactory	The nose and associated neuronal pathways and cortical areas
Tastes, flavors	Gustatory	The tongue, taste buds, and associated neuronal pathways and cortical areas

analyzed and the greatest proportion of speech communication is sent. As Mildred Freburg Berry points out,

> Audition, a primal modality, has a tonic influence upon the level of spontaneous activity in the entire brain. The spontaneous pattern goes on independently of the stimulation by sound. Loss of hearing, hence, is something more than the absence of stimulation—deafness. It means the loss of the spontaneous rhythm, a most important contributor to the "activity quotient" and stability of the central nervous system. If spontaneous rhythm in the auditory circuit is impaired, it could upset the stability of allied modalities.[6]

[3] This chart is unsophisticated in terms of physiology, chemistry, and physiological psychology. It is oversimplified to highlight those aspects of the subject which are of particular interest and use to the beginning student of speech communication.

[4] The modal analyzers can also be viewed as transducers, as end organs which apprehend one kind of input and transform it into another kind of stimulus. For example, the ear apprehends sound waves as waves of pressure and transforms these pressure waves into electrical impulses for neuronal transmission and cortical translation.

[5] Tactile/proprioceptive/kinesthetic—all differ slightly but all involve a stimulus of mechanical deformation, of pressure, either light or heavy. In general usage, taction implies touch on or outside the body of the subject, whereas proprioception and kinesthesia imply balance and pressure within the body of the subject. An individual touches another individual (tactile). An individual pays conscious attention to the action of his arm muscles in carrying a glass of water from a table to his mouth (proprioception). An individual is aware of visceral or abdominal rumblings and can feel definite pressures and movements within his abdomen (kinesthesia).

[6] *Language Disorders of Children* (New York: Appleton-Century-Crofts, 1969), pp. 38–39.

Many ideas concerning the auditory modality and the corresponding centrality of the spoken word may be found in Chapter 3. When words are spoken, auditory *and* kinesthetic *and* proprioceptive stimuli are all called into action and all reinforce one another. Very likely the reinforcement provided by these various modalities also creates a situation in which the sum is equal to more than the simple addition of all the parts. Recent experimental research reinforces the centrality of the spoken word when it finds that ". . . words said, will be remembered longer than words written, heard or read."[7]

Recall how when one is trying to repeat something from memory and forgets, he goes back to the beginning over and over hoping that the proprioception (motor memory) will take over and bridge the chasm of forgetfulness. The "memory of the muscles" is a way of characterizing proprioception. If you have ever played a piano, or almost any other musical instrument, you have probably experienced instances in which you block at a certain passage—and then try to overcome the block by starting from a point before it and playing with the hope that the muscle memory will carry you past the blocking point and enable you to continue with the rendition. The proprioceptive and kinesthetic modalities may well be among the most important for the development of speech communication. Pavlov and subsequent Soviet scholars suggest that the second signal system (man's speech communication) depends on such modalities. ". . . [S]peech . . . is . . . a kinesthetic stimulus going from the speech organs to the cortex. . . ."[8] Pavlov seems to be suggesting that the motor stimuli from the speech organs to the cortex are triggers for the process of speech communication and symbolization in the child. Such a position speaks to the possible importance of kinesthesia/ proprioception from the very outset of the individual's life. These modalities continue to play an important role throughout life. In later development of the child's ability to speak and to use speech communication, Luria notes,

> The development of the ability to perceive spoken sounds and to hear speech requires the closest participation of the articulatory apparatus and assumes its final character only in the process of active articulatory

[7] Loren D. Crane, Richard J. Dieker, and Charles T. Brown, "The Physiological Response to the Communication Modes: Reading, Writing, Speaking, and Evaluating," *The Journal of Communication*, Vol. 20, No. 3 (September 1970), 239.

[8] *A Handbook of Contemporary Soviet Psychology*, Michael Cole and Irving Maltzman, eds. (New York: Basic Books, Inc., Publishers, 1969), p. 68.

experience. The first years of development of speech are taken up with this acquisition of the ability to hear speech, with the participation of articulation.[9]

6.3. Seldom, if ever, does one mode have exclusivity. In the process of speech communication we find almost all the modes working simultaneously to reinforce or to contradict meaning. "Many sensory modalities—vision, olfaction, taction, audition, and proprioception— enter directly or indirectly into the comprehension—use of oral language."[10] We hear not only with our ears, but with our eyes as well. Recall instances when sound seems to interfere with visual concentration. When driving in heavy and confusing traffic, for example, many drivers find it helpful to turn off the radio to handle the many visual stimuli better. Similarly, when listening to a symphony, many people find it helpful to close their eyes. Marshall McLuhan discusses the interaction of visual and gustatory modalities in the decisions made by restaurant owners concerning decor and lighting.[11] Although we discuss each mode as if it could be operating alone, as practicing speech communicators we must always remember that the modes are most often operating simultaneously to reinforce or contradict one another. How often have we heard seemingly sincere words whose sincerity has been made dubious by the simultaneous cynical facial expression of the sender? At any given communicative moment one specific mode may be perceived as being dominant, but the dominant mode is always acting against a background of other modal activity. Varying modes (from a number of modes in action) can assert dominance at varying times across the chronology of a communication event. As indicated earlier, it *does* make a difference which mode is dominant since the various modes seem to carry differing emotional and cognitive weight in terms of communicative reception. Modal dominance is almost always purely relative. That at any moment one mode (such as vision) may seem to be carrying almost the total message is an illusion. Modes are almost invariably acting in concert, and although a specific mode may be

[9] Aleksandr Romanovich Luria, *Higher Cortical Functions in Man* (New York: Basic Books, Inc., Publishers, 1966), p. 102.

[10] Mildred Freburg Berry, *Language Disorders of Children* (New York: Appleton-Century-Crofts, 1969), p. 47.

[11] In Tom Wolfe, "What If He Is Right?" *The Pump House Gang* (New York: Bantam Books, Inc., 1968), pp. 105–33, *passim*.

perceived as dominant, its dominance is almost invariably projected against an active background of other modal activities.

The question of apparent dominance of activity should not be confused with the reality of the primal dominance of spoken speech communication—so flagged and identified by its meaningfulness in interpreting other modal forms and actions.

6.4. In considering modalities of speech communication, we can focus on the mode itself (for example, sound, light); on the mode as manifested in the activity of the speech communicator (for example, speaking, gesticulating); or on the mode as manifested in the activity of the receiver of the speech communication (for example, seeing, hearing). In much of the Soviet research the focus seems generally to be on the modes as manifested in the activity of the receiver of the speech communication. Such a focus results in a concentration of what may be referred to as "analyzers": the olfactory analyzer (smelling), the tactile and kinesthetic analyzers (feeling and touching), the auditory analyzer (hearing), and the visual analyzer (seeing). A stimulus may be perceived through more than one mode. A spoken word is usually heard; however, if the word is uttered with sufficient force or is electronically amplified, it may be felt as well as heard.

6.4.1. The modality analyzers play an active rather than a passive role in the process of communication. The ear does more than act as a passive sound receptor; the eye does more than act as a passive light receptor. At the moment of reception there simultaneously starts a process of analysis and synthesis. "... [S]ensation incorporates the process of analysis and synthesis of signals while they are still in the first stages of arrival."[12] In speaking of this same analytic/synthesizing phenomenon in vision, philosopher Remy Kwant observes,

> Through our seeing we actively constitute the world precisely as the field of vision. There is no question of merely receiving impressions . . . for, divorced from our seeing, there is no field of vision.[13]

[12] Luria, *op. cit.*, p. 97.
[13] Remy Kwant, *The Phenomenology of Expression* (Pittsburgh: Duquesne University Press, 1969), p. 24.

We do not see things in the same way as we hear or feel them. To know or understand something better we often try to apprehend it with as wide a variety of our modal analyzers as possible. We look at it, listen to it, touch it, smell it, and taste it. We use all appropriate analyzers because each one gives us different information concerning the object. Through the confluence of information fed from each analyzer we develop a fuller and more integrated way of "knowing" an object. The analyzer, the mode, plays a part in the perception of the object. Modal perception is *not* passive. The mode, to some extent, shapes the object perceived. Marshall McLuhan's aphorism, "The media is the message," speaks to this fact. In the act of perceiving the mode is not the totality of the message; but it is certainly part of the message, often an important part. If you envision a telescope as an extension of an eye (and consider the eye as part of the visual analyzer) and then look through the telescope (at either end), you will get the feeling of how a mode or modal analyzer can affect the thing perceived. Looking at the same object with the naked eye and then through both ends of the telescope confirms that the same external object is differently perceived depending on the mode of perception. The same is true of the other analyzers. Psychological factors can affect modal performance. Fear sometimes heightens the auditory analyzer so that what are normally meaningless and ignored sounds (a creaking chair, a water meter turning, a furnace starting up) are not only heard, but heard as much more discrete and intrusive sounds than normal. The tongue running around the inside of your mouth can find a small protrusion and magnify it into a major wound; looking inside your mouth with the aid of a mirror can place the magnitude of the wound in an altogether different perspective. All modes act on the external environment and affect, through their own characteristics, the meaning of what is transmitted to the brain for synthesis and action.

6.5. From the moment of reception the modes of communication affect the communication itself. In addition, a mode of communication can itself become a part of the communication or the message. The transformation from "mode" to "communication" is an instance of a medium becoming a message. In Chapter 1 the concepts of verbal/nonverbal and vocal/nonvocal are described briefly. Just as a stimulus can be at the same time verbal and nonvocal, so also can a stimulus be verbal and visual, verbal and tactile, and so on. Thus a touch can be verbally meaningful, as can a picture. When we recall the saying, "A picture is worth a thousand words," we must recall that a picture is worth a thousand words only if the viewer has at hand a thousand words with which to interpret the picture. Space can be verbally meaningful and space can be perceived visually (how far two speakers are from one another) and auditorially (the echo our voices create suggests the space in which we are speaking). How close to each other we stand when conversing may itself be an important part of the message. Are we angry with each other? fond of each other? Are we both of the same sex? Each question may be partially answered on the basis of the physical distance we maintain in conversation. Edward T. Hall has given specific attention to the meaningful role of personal and public space in human communication and has even developed an interpretive system which he labels "proxemics."[14] Professor Ray Birdwhistell has investigated the meaningfulness of small movements of the body or of parts of the body.[15] What is meant when a person raises an eyebrow, pulls down the corners of his mouth, crosses his legs at the ankles rather than at the knees, continuously pulls on an earlobe? The study of the meaning of such small movements within more general communicative contexts Birdwhistell calls "kinesics."

A popular report of the investigations of Birdwhistell, Hall, and other scientists with similar interests is provided in Julius Fast's book *Body Language.*[16] Fast defines body language as ". . . any nonreflexive or reflexive movement of a part, or all of the body, used by a person to communicate an emotional message to the outside world."[17] A summary of Hall's work is provided by Joseph DeVito in *The Psychology of Speech and Language.*[18] Whether you call it kinesics, proxemics, body language, or nonverbal communication, remember that almost any stimulus can carry symbolic or verbal meaning and that in most cases what is referred to as "nonverbal" really consists of nonvocal communicative stimuli. The modes of communication can themselves be communicative.

[14] Edward T. Hall, *The Silent Language* (Garden City, N. Y.: Doubleday & Company, Inc., 1959); and *The Hidden Dimension* (Garden City, N. Y.: Doubleday & Co., Inc., 1966).

[15] Ray L. Birdwhistell, *Kinesics and Context: Essays on Body Motion Communication* (Philadelphia: University of Pennsylvania Press, 1970); and "Certain Considerations on the Concepts of Culture and Communication," in *Perspectives on Communication*, Carl E. Larson and Frank E. X. Dance, eds. (Shorewood, Wis.: Helix Press, 1970), pp. 144–65.

[16] M. Evans & Co., Inc., and J. B. Lippincott Co. (Philadelphia and New York), 1970.

[17] *Ibid.*, pp. 10–11.

[18] (New York: Random House, Inc., 1970), pp. 82–83.

6.6. Obviously, modes are important since they offer the means by which speech communication is transmitted on any level. Intra-personally, kinesthesia, proprioception, and often audition as well as other modes can be operative. Interpersonally and person-to-persons, all modes may be operative. Since modes *mediate* the message and the meaning, modes can also *affect* the message and the meaning. Thus is it important that the speech communicator understand the modes of speech. It is better, in terms of expected and desired results, to have your speech communication modes reinforce each other rather than contradict or cancel one another. If you are uttering serious words, the visual stimuli (your gestures, your facial expression) should be appropriately serious.[19]

6.6.1. The speech communicator needs to be aware of what he is communicating through his various modalities during a communication event if he hopes to be able to make sensitive, accurate predictions of communication effectiveness. Just as you would be cautious, when trying to prove a point, not to use an example which contradicts the point you are trying to make, so should you be cautious not to send contradictory stimuli through various modalities. In *Presentation of Self in Everyday Life*, Erving Goffman suggests that when assessing the sincerity of a communicator, receivers are often on the lookout for modal contradictions in the communication event. A message, a meaning, a communicative event, gains credibility when there is cross-modal support, when a number of modalities reinforce each other. Credibility, either emotional or cognitive, may be strained by cross-modal contradiction. Cross-modal support and reinforcement can be a potent type of evidence. Modal evidence is more believable when it is appropriate to the mode in use (visual evidence for the visual mode, auditory evidence for the auditory mode); when the modal evidence is not contradictory (when visual evidence is not contradicted by auditory evidence); and when there is little suspicion of modal distortion (when the receiver does not feel that the sender is trying to distort the modal evidence or is taking advantage of illusions, for example, trying to suggest certain relationships through colors on a chart with the hope that the

---

[19] This is not to say that you cannot consciously make good use of modal contradiction. The contradiction of the clown costume and makeup with the pathos of the sung message in *Pagliacci* and Barbra Streisand's melancholic rendition of "Happy Days Are Here Again" both testify to the effectiveness of a planned modal contradiction in performance. But these are planned, not accidental or uncontrolled examples.

emotional overtones certain colors suggest would affect the logic of the argument). Another example of modal evidence is trying to "bully" the auditory modality by force, volume, or mumbling so that meaning is clouded and possibly misunderstood.

There is something discomfiting about a relationship in which a person who says he loves you is unwilling to touch or be touched by you. What is wrong may or may not be connected with the objective truth of the statement (one of the people involved may have a skin disease, or may by prior psychological conditioning be unable to tolerate *anyone* touching him; but something is still wrong. In such a case the auditory modality is challenged by the tactile modality, creating a dissonance which calls for resolution. We can build support for our message by using modal cross-referencing. When we *say* something we can try, if possible, to *act* it out as well. If we say "I really like the tie you gave me," we can add to the credibility of our message by wearing the tie, giving cross-modal visual support to our acoustic message.

6.7. The search for valid cross-modal support leads to the use of audio-visual aids in speech communication. Audio-visual aids lend emphasis and extension to spoken communication. In almost every case the audio-visual aid is an extension of the spoken word rather than a substitution for it. For example, a speaker can certainly recite a list of numerals, a set of statistical points, or a recapitulation of a census, but it is almost impossible for the average auditor to retain these lists of figures in his auditory memory for any significant length of time. If part of the impact of the speech depends on the audience's remembering sets of figures for the purpose of analysis and comparison, it is essential that some means be provided for the audience to make or have a record of the figures before them. In such a case a visual aid, a printed handout, or a blackboard listing would be helpful. If your speech makes use of lengthy quotations or references for support or illustration, it is useful to have such materials available in mimeographed or dittoed form for audience retention following the actual speech. If your speech deals with contemporary trends in music or in art, recordings or slides would be appropriate. Slides, tape recordings, disc recordings, handouts, blackboards, and transparencies are examples of audio-visual aids. Obviously, each of these instruments provides an opportunity for cross-modal referencing and support.

SUMMARY

1. The modes, the methods through which speech communication is manifested, are auditory, kinesthetic/proprioceptive, olfactory, tactile, and visual.

2. Modes are determined by human physiological and neurological capabilities.

3. Seldom does one mode have exclusivity—usually we find almost all modes working simultaneously.

4. It makes a difference which mode is dominant since different modes seem to carry different emotional and cognitive weight in terms of communication reception.

5. Modality analyzers play an active rather than a passive role in the process of communication.

6. A mode of communication can itself become a part of the communication, a part of the message.

7. Cross-modal support and reinforcement can be a potent type of evidence.

8. Audio-visual aids lend emphasis and extension to spoken communication.

EXERCISES

1. (a) Prepare and deliver a short speech in which you try to use but a single modality.
   (b) Based on your speech for part (a), discuss the following points:
      (i) To what degree were you successful in using a single modality?
      (ii) What effect did the modal dominance have on the effectiveness of the speech?
      (iii) In what kinds of communicative events, if any, would modal dominance be helpful? Harmful?

2. Carefully plan and enact a speech communication event in which cross-modal contradiction is used to achieve a specific purpose.

3. Marshall McLuhan states "The medium is the message." Construct and enact a speech communication event in which a mode of communication becomes a part of the message.

ADDITIONAL READINGS

Andrew, Richard J., "The Origins of Facial Expression," *Scientific American*, Vol. 213, No. 4 (Oct. 1965), 88–94.

Fischhoff, Joseph, "Family Disturbances and Children's Non-Verbal Behavior," *Medical Times*, Vol. 94, No. 2 (February 1966), 151–56.

Knapp, Mark L., *Nonverbal Communication in Human Interaction*. New York: Holt, Rinehart and Winston, Inc., 1972.

LaBarre, Weston, "The Cultural Basis of Emotions and Gestures," *Journal of Personality*, Vol. 16 (September 1947), 49–68.

McLuhan, Marshall, *Understanding Media*. New York: McGraw-Hill Book Company, 1964.

Milner, Peter M., *Physiological Psychology*. New York: Holt, Rinehart and Winston, Inc., 1970. Especially Part 3, Sensory Systems.

Rosenblith, Walter A., *Sensory Communication*. New York: John Wiley & Sons, Inc., 1961.

Smith, Alfred G., *Communication and Culture*. New York: Holt, Rinehart and Winston, Inc., 1966.

Chapter 7

SPEECH

COMMUNICATION

AND

ROLES

Conceptual Term: **ROLE**

Conceptual Description. *". . . [T]he pattern of expectations regarding the occupant of a position."*[1]

Discussion. *Role is a socially determined set of expectations for the behavior of individuals who hold certain positions within a society, organization, or group. Other descriptions of the concept of role state:*

". . . a functionally real social category"[2];
". . . role refers to the set of expectations which group members share concerning the behavior of a person who occupies a given position in the group."[3]

Examples. *Occupational roles: teacher, doctor; kinship roles: mother, brother; age roles: child, teen-ager, "golden-ager"; sex roles: male, female.*

7.1. Like other fruitful concepts, "role" has spawned a number of ancillary concepts which

[1] Dean Barnlund, *Interpersonal Communication* (Boston: Houghton Mifflin Company, 1968), p. 159.
[2] Roger Brown, *Social Psychology* (New York: The Free Press, 1965), p. 135.
[3] A. Paul Hare, *Handbook of Small Group Research* (New York: The Free Press, 1962), p. 101.

extend the usefulness of the original idea. Viewed together, all the applications of the concept of role and of its extensions offer the student a way of interpreting much of human behavior. Since such an interpretation exhibits a certain consistency of viewpoint, it has come to be called *role theory*. Role itself does not determine how a person in a given situation will fulfill the *role expectations*, or the way in which other members of the group expect him to behave if he is to fill the role satisfactorily. A person's behavior in acting out a role may be called either *role enactment* or *role performance*. The manner in which he fulfills more than one role determines his *role versatility*. The way in which he moves from one role to another is labeled *role transition*. The number of roles he can enact or perform constitutes his *role repertoire* or *role repertory*.

Often we have been told to "try to look at the problem from my point of view." We have also heard the statement that it is important from time to time to "try to walk in the other man's shoes." The idea behind both of these injunctions is that it helps in adjusting to society and to life if you can from time to time "get out of yourself" and see how the world looks to others. This theme also underlies the suggestion sometimes given in discussions and arguments that before replying to a statement made by one of the other persons in the discussion you must repeat that person's argument *to his satisfaction*. In other words, you must show him that you fully understand his argument and the rationale underlying it before you state your position on the point at issue. Such an exercise, which often helps reduce tension and increase understanding, forces you to suspend your own biases at least long enough to grasp the other person's argument in sufficient detail to restate it to his satisfaction. When you restate the argument from your opponent's viewpoint, you are engaged in *role taking*; you project yourself, as completely as possible, into the role of the other individual.[4]

---

[4] It is important to make the distinction between "role" and "personality." You can try to place yourself in the role of another person without taking on his personality. You may be a student trying to see things from the point of view of a teacher, or a son or daughter trying to see things from the point of view of a parent. The role of teacher or parent will be filled by you with *your* personality. The same role can be filled by different individuals with different personalities. You can see a play or a movie many times, each time with a different cast: the same play or movie with the same roles, but with different actors having different personalities acting out the roles. Indeed, the changing personalities in the unchanging roles are often what proves the artistic excellence of a play.

7.2. Evidence suggests that there is a marked correspondence between role-taking skills and human communication skills. A recent series of studies indicates that a child's skill in human communication is directly correlated with his skill in role taking.[5] Taking his original research cues from the writings of Jean Piaget, Flavell and his associates proposed a model of human communication that involves a primary coding of a message by a speaker and then, *before the message is sent*, a recoding of the same message from the point of view of the receiver. In other words, the success of the message— gauged by the receiver's ability to respond in a manner identical to or close to that in which the speaker wished him to respond—is directly related to the capacity of the speaker to understand the receiver's point of view, or role, and to recast his own primary coded message in light of the receiver's role. As Flavell says,

> An important part of what is involved in effective communicating might be conceptualized as a coding-then-recoding process, in which the recoding component is "monitored," so to speak, by role-taking activity.[6]

Piaget, primarily a developmental psychologist, has dealt extensively with the role of egocentricity in child development. Egocentricity can interfere with the capacity to take on oneself another's role. Thus, it could be suggested that role-taking capacity and egocentricity vary in indirect ratio and that this variance affects the individual's success in human communication. However, the ability to participate accurately in role taking is not in itself either a sufficient or necessary condition for successful communication. The speaker might be extremely sensitive and accurate in his role-taking capabilities but unable to communicate successfully because of some inadequacy in his perceptual, cognitive, or physiological equipment. In such a case the speaker's role-taking capacities will be insufficient to guarantee him communicative success. As another example, two individuals might be so delicately attuned to one another that the primary coding of the speaker is almost identical to the primary coding of the receiver, eliminating the need for the recoding step in sending the message. In this case, which rarely occurs in ordinary life,

---

[5] John H. Flavell, *The Development of Role-Taking and Communication Skills in Children* (New York: John Wiley & Sons, Inc., 1968).
[6] *Ibid.*, p. 8.

role-taking capability seems to be unnecessary. In most human communication the ability to discriminate the other's role attributes accurately is invaluable in developing the capacity to behave appropriately toward him within the constraints of your own role.

In Chapter 4 we discussed the levels of speech communication. In treating level one, intrapersonal speech communication (see Section 4.2), the point was made that we communicate within ourselves and that two or more individuals are not necessary for speech communication. Indeed, we do carry on speech communication intrapersonally, but that communication always posits some intrapersonal role distinction. We talk to ourselves from different positions: first we are the proponent of an argument, then we oppose the same argument, and our intrapersonal speech communication alternates in a dialogue between these two roles, both played by the same individual with the same personality. Obviously, interpersonal speech communication (level two) involves role discrimination, role taking, and role enactment (see Section 4.2.2), since to communicate effectively with another we must be adept at discriminating that other's role attributes and at recoding our messages in terms of those role attributes. Person-to-persons speech communication (see Section 4.2.3) also involves roles. The most obvious level three roles are those of "speaker" and of "member of an audience."

Roles can affect all three levels of speech communication. The system of levels is dynamically interrelated (see Section 4.3), and thus the effect of role can move in either direction, from level three back through levels two and one, or from level one through levels two and three.

The prolonged enactment of a certain role may affect the personality of the individual filling that role. Someone who has for an extended time filled the role of an authoritarian leader may find his personality becoming more and more authoritarian. This change in personality will in due course lead to level one changes, which will then be transmitted through levels two and three. The original role enactment may have been on level two or three, later affecting level one and finally being formalized in the individual's total level two and three speech communication behavior. As another example, an individual may develop hallucinations which lead to certain level one role enactments and speech communication patterns, as in some cases of paranoia or schizophrenia. In such instances the communication patterns will in turn manifest themselves in level two and level three speech communication behavior. People can come to believe their own roles, to believe their own publicity. Everyday experience brings each of us into contact with someone we classify as "stuck-up," who has succumbed to his identification of personality with role. Evidence of this tendency is also found in public figures who seem to undergo a metamorphosis upon the assumption of public office or upon the sudden acquisition of fame because of theatrical, sports, or intellectual success. Such individuals suddenly become untouchable and give cues that they see themselves now as above the "masses," entitled to deferential treatment. Thus can role affect personality.

The relationship between role and personality is intimate, interesting, and can work both ways. "People are attracted toward positions which will suit their particular personalities; for example students high in authoritarianism find their way towards military academies."[7] We have already given anecdotal support for the effect of role on personality. However, available research evidence also testifies to the effect of role on behavior. Playing a role can affect a person's view of himself. There have been fictitious treatments of this theme, as when an actor playing the stage role of a murderer ends up becoming a murderer in real life. Another example is that of the prince and the pauper, in which the pauper, who by agreement is playing the role of the prince for one night, becomes reluctant to give up the position and all of its perquisites. In an interesting research examination of the effect of role on human behavior, E. P. Torrance tested problem solving in bomber crews consisting of a pilot, navigator, and gunner.[8]

> He found that members of these crews influenced the crew's decision in strict accordance with their rank and power. As a consequence, when the correct answer to a problem was held by a person with little power, the crew was less likely to reach a correct group answer than when a powerful person had the correct answer.[9]

The rank and power of the various crew members in the Torrance

[7] Michael Argyle, *Social Interaction* (Chicago: Aldine-Atherton, Inc., 1969), p. 279.

[8] Torrance, E. P., "Some Consequences of Power Differences on Decision Making in Permanent and Temporary Three-Man Groups," *Research Studies, State College of Washington*, Vol. 22 (1954), pp. 130–40.

[9] Dorwin Cartwright and Alvin Zander, eds., *Group Dynamics: Research and Theory* (2nd ed.) (New York: Harper and Row, Publishers, 1960), p. 662.

study were related directly to their roles rather than to their personalities, and the study gives evidence of how role affects behavior.

Role affects behavior, and behavior often shapes personality. We are what we have done and we shall become what we will do. Action shapes being. An individual who starts riding horses at an early age and continues to do so throughout his formative years may acquire bowed legs from his activity. Someone who continually carries heavy weights in one hand may find that arm becoming longer than the other. In such physical examples, once the legs are bowed or the arm is made longer, the cessation of the activity will not always result in the return of the body to its prior state. In instances where actions have shaped mental or emotional states, retraining is possible, though sometimes long and difficult. Someone who begins to suspect others of wanting to do him ill may, if he continues this pattern, become enduringly suspicious of everyone. If you wish to become a baseball player or a bridge player, you engage in playing baseball or bridge. Action shapes being.[10] Behavior shapes personality, and role affects behavior.

In Chapter 1 the concept of the significant symbol was described and briefly discussed. The creation of significant symbols is the product of role taking. Through taking the role of others during the stages of our own symbol formation we develop the capacity to respond to symbols as others respond to them. The common response to a symbol, which imbues the symbol with significance, depends on a certain level of sophistication in role taking.

An understanding of this relationship may provide some additional help in discriminating between animal communication and human communication. Can we ever expect an animal, other than the human animal, to take on itself the role of responding other? No research suggests that the animal can engage in a role-taking pattern. The animal codes only for itself; no evidence suggests that an animal message sender ever recodes the message in terms of the other animal to which the message is directed. In Chapter 3 we presented an argument concerning the centrality of the spoken word in human communication. Mead seems to be speaking to this point when he states,

[10] A fuller development of this idea may be found in Frank E. X. Dance, "Performance as Content in Speech Communication Education," *The Central States Speech Journal*, Vol. XIX, No. 3 (Fall 1968), 175–84.

...it is only the vocal gesture to which one responds or tends to respond as another person responds to it. It is true that the language of the hands is of the same character. One sees one's self using the gestures which those who are deaf make use of. They influence one the same way as they influence others. Of course, the same is true of any form of script. *Such symbols have all been developed out of the specific vocal gesture, for that is the basic gesture which does influence the individual as it influences others.* [11]

It becomes increasingly evident that the concepts of role and of human speech communication are closely intertwined both in development and in practice.

In examining the levels of human communication we sometimes have the implicit feeling that it is harder to successfully disguise level one communication than the communication which is observed on levels two or three. Perhaps this is because roles are more easily called into action on levels two and three than on level one. When communicating on level two or three an individual can easily ascribe his communicative behavior, in some part at least, to the role expectations operating in the situation. In level one communication we are supposedly dealing without much role intervention. In reality, even on level one we tend to allow roles to affect our communicative behavior. As mentioned earlier, we can come to believe our own role publicity in a manner that leads us to talk even to ourselves within role patterns.

Role is an essentially impersonal concept when compared with the concepts of person and of personality. In many situations we feel slighted when we perceive that someone is communicating with us as a "role" rather than as a "person." The successful communicator knows when it is appropriate to engage primarily in inter-role communication and when it is appropriate and desirable to communicate primarily interpersonally. Too often a confusion of role and person leads to breakdowns in communication. In the academic setting, for example, an individual plays the role of student or professor. In certain cases the student may expect the professor to relate to him not as a student but as a person and a friend, and be confused when the professor maintains the professorial role. The

[11] George H. Mead, "Language and the Development of the Self," in *Readings in Social Psychology*, Theodore M. Newcomb and Eugene L. Harley, eds. (New York: Holt, Rinehart and Winston, Inc., 1947), p. 182. Italics added.

professor, on the other hand, finds it difficult to indicate to the student-friend when it is appropriate to maintain the student–professor role relationship and when it is appropriate to enter into the friend–friend relationship. Such role confusion or *role conflict* on the part of an individual in a relationship can lead to serious communication difficulties if not correctly perceived and successfully dealt with. Generally speaking, it seems more desirable to engage in interpersonal communication, with due understanding of the varieties of role relationships existing, than to engage in inter-role communication while suppressing the interpersonal dimension.

7.3. Speech communication plays an important part in confirming identity. Through the mechanisms of role taking and the significant symbol, speech communication is constantly involved in the individual's confirmation of self. Mead says, "Selves can only exist in definite relationship to other selves."[12]

The confirmation of self, the construction and acceptance of an identity, is essential to individual development, maturity, and happiness. It has often been argued that one of the most difficult phases in the maturing process occurs when the adolescent is trying to escape his identity as "dependent" and successfully enter a new identity as "independent." Life is filled with many such changes: from "student" to "professor," from "child" to "parent," from "single" to "married." How one talks to himself and to others plays a large and important part in the confirmation of self and in the transition to new identities. Obviously, as we grow older we take on new roles. Each suggests a different way of engaging in speech communication on all three levels. Indeed, if we fail to engage in appropriate level one communication it is likely that this failure will also be projected to levels two and three, with possible concomitant communication difficulties. In like manner we must adjust our communication to others in terms of their changing age. In this way, through our level two communication we help confirm the level one communication of others, and they do the same for us.

The opposite of self-confirmation is disconfirmation of self. Disconfirmation of self can be psychologically damaging. The person who considers himself mature and independent but whom others communicate with as if he were immature and dependent must

[12] *Ibid.*, p. 189.

reconcile this contradiction. The reconciliation may, because of physical or social pressure, be able to be made only at the cost of disconfirmation of self, which can be so psychologically harmful that the individual is handicapped in dealing both with himself and with others for many years—in some instances, for the rest of his life. Examples of the way in which speech communication can be used either to confirm or to disconfirm self abound: the parent who says to his child, "You can do it, you've got the brains to get a good grade," versus the parent who says, "Dummy, I've always told you you were too stupid to make it through school"; the bigot who calls a fully grown man "Boy" for the sole purpose of damaging the man's self-image. It has been said that a manner of speaking can become a way of thinking. That is true. A person can talk himself into, or out of, almost anything. The potency of speech communication in the confirmation of self provides at least one part of the argument for the ethical use of speech communication by everyone.

> Every man is a potential adversary, even those whom we love. Only through dialogue are we saved from this enmity toward one another. Dialogue is to love, what blood is to the body. When the flow of blood stops, the body dies. When dialogue stops, love dies and resentment and hate are born. But dialogue can restore a dead relationship. Indeed, this is the miracle of dialogue: it can bring relationship into being, and it can bring into being once again a relationship that has died.[13]

Howe's dialogue is very similar to the idea of openness in interpersonal communication. Role can often interpose itself in such a way as to hinder rather than facilitate interpersonal communication. Some people seek escape from personhood in the roles they play. A sad but pointed example of such escape through role is the effort of certain military personnel to disclaim their personal responsibility for atrocities against other people by appealing to their military role duties. Two of the characteristics of our time are the increasing reluctance of many people to accept such excuses and the renewed emphasis on the importance of person and personhood. In dialogical communication individuals are challenged to suppress those elements which would make the meeting of persons difficult.

---

[13] Reuel L. Howe, *The Miracle of Dialogue* (New York: The Seabury Press, Inc., 1963), p. 3.

Dialogue is that address and response between persons in which there is a flow of meaning between them in spite of all the obstacles that normally would block the relationship. It is that interaction between persons in which one of them seeks to give himself as he is to the other, and seeks also to know the other as the other is. This means that he will not attempt to impose his own truth and view on the other. Such is the relationship which characterizes dialogue and is the precondition to dialogical communication.[14]

The voluntary divesting of role is threatening for many individuals because they have, through habit, become so closely identified with their role. We are born into roles: the age role of infant, the kinship role of son or daughter, the economic role of dependent. It is easy to confuse our roles with our persons. We are protected against such over-identification during youth by the constant need to change roles. We move through so many different age roles and we acquire new relational roles (husband/wife) that the constant challenge of role transition prevents most of us from becoming fixated on any one of the early roles we play. However, as we eventually assume roles for extended periods of time (doctor, lawyer, teacher, artist, rich man, wife) we may well find ourselves identifying more and more with the role to the exclusion of other elements of our personhood. The individual who plays the role of professor so constantly that he becomes pompous and pedantic in almost all of his communicative behavior is an example of the merging of one's personhood with one's role. Especially when the role brings ceremonious honors, such as the role of public official, military officer or religious leader, it is easy to confuse self with role. Role rigidity, the inability to move from role to role or to abstract oneself from roles from time to time, is dangerous to the functioning of a wholesome personality and to the maintenance of normal human relationships. The individual who is fixed in a certain role finds it difficult, if not impossible, to look at things from the other's point of view. Since role taking is so directly connected with communication success, such role rigidity would seem to preclude sensitive and successful interpersonal communication.

In certain schools of acting beginning actors were encouraged to "live the role." The idea seemed to be for the actor to so submerge himself in the role that he ceased to be himself at all and became the

[14] *Ibid.*, p. 37.

role. Such a process is dubious for the actor and dangerous for everyone. A role is not a person; when the two become confused, so do the life and the communication of the person playing the role. *At all times a person should be in control of his roles rather than the role or roles being in control of the person*. We should be able to step into and out of the various roles we play and to know when it is appropriate to assume the various role behaviors open to us. "It is a widely accepted postulate that the more roles in a person's behavior repertory, the 'better' his social adjustment—other things being equal."[15] What human communicators should strive for is as widely developed a role repertory as possible. At all times each of us should know the answer to the question "Who is in control of your behavior, the role, or you?"

7.4. Role plays a significant part in speech communication behavior. In an earlier chapter we discussed the concept of inner speech and its part in the functions of speech communication. Flavell's idea of a coding/recoding model suggests an additional way of viewing the distinction between inner and external speech. Since inner speech is coded for self and not for others, the recoding step is short-circuited and inner speech fails to be affected by the recoding occasioned by role taking prior to message sending. The previous discussion of the possible effects of role on level one speech communication behavior also has implications for speech communication on other levels and in all of its functions.

How we talk to ourselves affects how we talk to others. How we view various roles affects how we shape our expectations for the speech communication of others. Expectations play a great part in speech communication effectiveness. Often we hear what we want to hear, and what we want and expect to hear is shaped by our role expectations for both the speaker and the listener. If we conceive our role to be such that we feel we should be treated with deference and respect, and our communication partner perceives us as an "old buddy" and communicates with us using the informal grammar and vocabulary typical of warm and old friends, there is a great likelihood of a communication breakdown. The expectations created by role are dissonant.

[15] Theodore R. Sarbin, "Role Theory," in *Handbook of Social Psychology*, Vol. I, Gardner Lindzey, ed. (Reading, Mass.: Addison-Wesley Publishing Co., Inc., 1954), pp. 223–58.

The tradition of the importance of the first impression finds some rationale in role behavior and communication. When we meet someone for the first time we are alert to cues revealing how he views himself and what role he is playing, and we too are usually giving out role cues. If our first role impression of the other is of an overly serious, professorial type, those cues may shape our communicative behavior for a long time to come. Conversely, our unconscious cues revealing our conception of our role will shape the communicative behavior of the other in the same fashion.

The classical concept of "ethos," of what a person brings to a communicative situation outside of the specific message peculiar to the communicative moment; and the contemporary concept of "source credibility," of how believable and trustworthy a person is, are also clarified by role theory. Ethos and source credibility are often attached to the role rather than to the person. In experimental research, the same message has been attributed to two speakers who differed in terms of role. If, for instance, the message dealt with national health policies, one speaker might be identified as the surgeon general of the United States and the second speaker as a college student. In such an instance role expectations for the two speakers enhanced the ethos and source credibility of one over the other. Role and ethos, and role and source credibility, are related.

Roles and stereotypes have some things in common, but they also have some essential differences. Whereas roles shape expectations, stereotypes are so strong as to be almost prescriptive. "All Irishmen are hard drinkers" may be so strong a stereotype for some that they find it impossible to conceive of an Irishman who is not a drinking man and they will project their stereotype onto the Irish regardless of behavioral evidence to the contrary. Stereotypes also have more personal connotations than do roles. Stereotypes seem to suggest similar personal qualities, whereas roles can be filled by individuals with differing personalities. Obviously, stereotypes play a real part in the shaping of communicative behavior on both the interpersonal and the person-to-persons levels.

In level three communication we are often encouraged to analyze our audience with as much accuracy as possible. During the process of growing up most of us have been constantly engaged in audience analysis. Actually, the whole process of role taking is a miniature model of audience analysis. In role taking we are trying to "get inside" our listener, to assess how our communication will affect him, and to determine how it can best be adjusted to his needs and expectations. In level three audience analysis we are trying to do the same thing for many listeners. The natural beginning, the normal starting point for audience analysis, is self-analysis.

In the creation of our "self" we have continually engaged in role taking and in audience analysis. Therefore, in preparing for any level three communication we should start by analyzing how we ourselves would view the situation and would be affected by any particular communicative behavior sequence. Since the individual is in some ways a microcosm of all the responding others with whom he has had contact in the course of his development, he has within him great resources for audience analysis.

The great to-do about listening in contemporary communication literature also may be clarified by relating it to what we have learned about role theory and speech communication. When we really "listen" we are listening not just as ourselves but as the others with whom we are in communication. We are listening to the other's role, the other's person, as well as to his words. In real listening we are engaged in dialogue at all times. When we listen only in a given role, then we filter out much that we would hear were we listening in a different role. The same communicative structure, when listened to in the role of "enemy," may carry an entirely different message than if it were listened to in the role of "lover." This suggests the importance of trying to listen as a person rather than as a role. Just as we should engage in interpersonal rather than inter-role speech communication, so should we engage in interpersonal rather than inter-role listening. The wide variety of prescriptive advice for improving listening can generally be reduced to "pay attention" and "try to find areas of common interest between what is being said and your own activities." The active practice of role taking may now be added to suggestions on how to improve our understanding and retention of the communication of others.

Feedback overlaps with listening. When we speak of feedback we are generally referring to the assessment of the success or failure of our past communicative behavior and the consequent altering of our future communicative behavior.

Obviously, the garnering of feedback is related to listening but is not completely identical with listening. Feedback may be silent, completely visual (the nodding of heads in either agreement or weariness), tactile (a slap on the back or an embrace); feedback can take many forms. The accurate perception and assessment of feedback also depends on sensitivity and capability in role taking. How do we know what certain visual stimuli emitted by others mean unless we are skilled in taking the role of the other? The development of facile and accurate feedback skills is related to the possession and use of accurate role-taking skills. What is more, feedback and role taking are mutually developmental, that is, the development of one enhances the development of the other. The accurate perception of feedback enables us to make judgments of the role attributes of those with whom we are communicating as well as to make decisions concerning our own role-taking behavior relative to those with whom we are communicating.

Flavell and Piaget both discuss the part played by egocentricity in role taking and speech communication.[16] The capacity of an individual to abstract from himself, to lay aside his own needs and desires and take on the point of view of another, is related to his role-taking capacity and to his communication effectiveness. Children find such "decentering," or laying aside of themselves as the center of their attention and universe, very difficult. Only with experience and sensitivity do most of us develop the capacity to see things from the other person's point of view. The individual who has developed this decentering capacity often finds it difficult to understand the communication behavior of someone who has not yet developed the ability. Perhaps this explains in part the inability of the adolescent and the adult to understand each other as completely as both suggest is desirable. The adult who has developed a capacity to decenter is bewildered by what he interprets as the "selfishness" of the adolescent. That "selfishness" may, however, simply reflect the incomplete development of the adolescent's ability to decenter and thus his inability to take on himself the role of the adult in his interpersonal communication behavior.

Role theory has application to speech communication on all three levels and in all three functions. Role theory is a good example of the fact that a theory, an idea, or a hunch can have value and utility without being proven.

[16] Flavell, *op. cit.*

SUMMARY

1. Role is the pattern of expectations regarding the occupant of a position.

2. Role is socially determined.

3. In the process of role taking you project yourself as completely as possible into the role of another individual.

4. There seems to be a marked correspondence of role-taking skills and human communication skills.

5. Intrapersonal communication posits intrapersonal role distinctions.

6. The prolonged enactment of a certain role may affect the personality of the individual filling the role.

7. The creation of significant symbols is the product of role taking.

8. Confusion between role and person can lead to breakdowns in speech communication.

9. Through the mechanisms of role taking and the significant symbol, speech communication plays an important part in the confirming of identity.

10. The confirmation of self is essential to individual development, maturity, and happiness.

11. The miracle of open interpersonal speech communication—of dialogue—is that it can bring relationship into being and can, in fact, bring into being once again a relationship that has died.

12. Role rigidity is dangerous to the functioning of a wholesome personality and to the maintenance of normal human relationships.

13. We should strive for as widely developed a role repertory as possible.

14. At all times you, rather than your role, should be in control of your behavior.

15. Role, ethos, and source credibility are interrelated.

16. In the creation of our "self" we have continuously engaged in role taking and thus in audience analysis.

17. The active practice of role taking may improve our understanding and retention of the communication of others—our "listening."

18. Feedback and role taking are mutually related and mutually developmental.

EXERCISES

1. Making notes on your results, interview three adolescents, three adults, and three people over 60 years of age. Ask each individual the same question: "Who are you?" Try not to lead the respondent in any specific direction in giving his answer. What you are investigating is the degree to which individuals in different age groups identify with varying roles. In other words, do they simply give you their name, their job title, their professional identification, or their family role (grandfather, husband, or the like), or are their answers more complicated, taking into consideration a number of roles played as well as other personal values? Prepare to report your findings to the class, drawing whatever conclusion you feel is appropriate from your brief research task.

2. Can it be said that animals other than humans ever play roles? If so, give examples and an explanation. If not, why not?

3. The following case is based on a factual report.

> A Peace Corps volunteer had served more than two years overseas when he learned of compelling personal reasons demanding his return home. He asked his Peace Corps representative (his immediate superior) what the policy was on leaving two months earlier than his agreed six-months extension date. The representative said, "No problem, you write home and say you'll be there in two weeks." Happily the volunteer began to tie up his work. He wrote home and received replies expressing relief that he was able to return home. He went in for his termination physical examination and saw the same Peace Corps representative once again.
> This time the Peace Corps representative screamed that the only way the volunteer could leave early was to resign, otherwise it would be favoritism. When the volunteer pointed out that the representative himself had suggested that there was no difficulty in arranging the early termination, the representative responded by giving the volunteer a long speech on the Greek word for courage. At no time, even after several questions, would the representative give any reasons for changing his mind. The representative kept repeating, "Put your money where your mouth is—quit!"
> The volunteer felt he had put too much time and effort into his Peace Corps experience to resign from it; however, his family expected him home for reasons which could really wait two months, but only at the risk of becoming much more critical by that time.
> The representative refused to discuss the matter further.

(a) Using what you know about the correspondence of role theory and effective speech communication, prepare an analysis of the case, stating why you think the communication breakdown occurred and what you feel could be done to solve the difficulty.

(b) Choose a partner from the members of the class. One of you take the role of the volunteer and the other the role of the representative. Start the role playing as the volunteer approaches the representative one last time to try to find out what has caused the representative to change his mind.

(c) Switch roles and play the incident again.

4. Role play a conversation between a professor and a student in which the student is asking for a chance to raise his course grade by doing extra work.

(a) *Role play I.*   The professor is the student's father.

(b) *Role play II.*   The student and the professor are in the same National Guard unit. The student is a captain and the professor is a sergeant.

ADDITIONAL READINGS

Barnlund, Dean, *Interpersonal Communication: Survey and Studies.* Boston: Houghton Mifflin Company, 1968, pp. 151–73.

Biddle, Bruce J., and Edwin J. Thomas, eds., *Role Theory: Concepts and Research.* New York: John Wiley & Sons, Inc., 1966.

Houle, Cyril O., *The Inquiring Mind.* Madison, Wis.: University of Wisconsin Press, 1961.

Jourard, Sidney M., *The Transparent Self.* New York: Van Nostrand Reinhold Company, 1964.

Piaget, Jean, *The Language and Thought of the Child.* New York: World Publishing Co., 1962.

Tournier, Paul, *The Meaning of Persons.* New York: Harper and Row, Publishers, 1957.

Chapter 8

THE

INTRAPERSONAL

LEVEL

8.1. A proper point of departure for our discussion of the intrapersonal level is provided by Barker and Wiseman.

Intrapersonal communication refers to the creating, the functioning, and evaluating of symbolic processes which operate primarily within oneself. Levels of intrapersonal communication range along a continuum according to the extent messages are stored in the environment around the self communication system. Such activities as "thinking," "meditating," and "reflecting," which may require no environmental storage outside the life space of the communicator, are on one end of this continuum and activities such as "talking aloud to oneself" and "writing oneself a note," which require considerably more environmental storage, are on the other end of this continuum.[1]

Figure 8.1 represents the model advanced by Barker and Wiseman to describe, in general terms, the phenomena involved in intrapersonal communication.

8.1.1. This model, and Barker and Wiseman's explication of it, call to our attention a number of relevant observations about the

[1] Larry L. Barker and Gordon Wiseman, "A Model of Intrapersonal Communication," *Journal of Communication*, 16 (1966), 174.

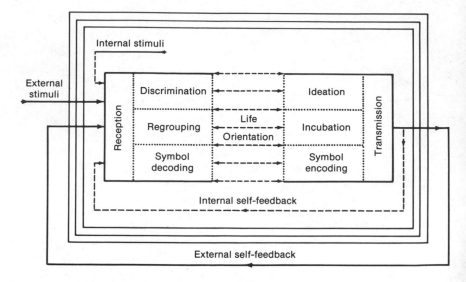

FIGURE 8.1 Barker and Wiseman's intrapersonal communication model.

nature of intrapersonal communication. First, we note that a single individual is both the origin and destination of intrapersonal messages. In Chapter 2 we said that the sufficient condition for intrapersonal communication is the attaching of meaning or significance to any externally or internally generated stimulus. Thus, the intrapersonal communication model allows us to take into account phenomena which occur externally, in addition to stimuli generated internally. Interestingly, we are capable of processing internally generated stimuli as if they were "real" externally generated stimuli. A second observation focuses on the two types of self-feedback. Internal self-feedback occurs when messages which are generated internally are received "covertly, through bone conduction, muscular contractions, or neuro circuitry in the central nervous system."[2] External self-feedback occurs when messages are received overtly, through the sensory receptor organs. In other words, we are capable of monitoring messages we produce, in some cases by "hearing ourselves talk," and in other cases by attending to our own thoughts.

8.1.2. At the reception phase of intrapersonal communication the individual is confronted with great numbers of internally and externally generated stimuli. Most of these stimuli are screened out

[2] Barker and Wiseman, p. 177.

(discrimination), the ones which are consciously attended to are ordered according to their strength (regrouping), and meaning is attached to a stimulus or configurations of stimuli (symbol decoding). These processes occur almost simultaneously; their particular forms are influenced heavily by the "life orientation" of the communicator. Later in this chapter we shall discuss some of the more common influences of life orientations on intrapersonal communication processes.

8.1.3. At the transmission phase of intrapersonal communication, the stimuli which have already been decoded symbolically are given shape or form (ideation), are allowed to "jell" for a period of time which may range from a fraction of a second to a lifetime (incubation), and then from the almost infinite number of messages which might be formulated to represent these residual thoughts, a given message is formulated (symbol encoding).

The model is a general one intended to represent intrapersonal communication phenomena ranging from covert thought to overt speech. Let us now examine more specifically the role of speech in intrapersonal communication.

8.2. Intrapersonal Speech Communication. We have chosen to view speech communication as the process, or the product of the process, of the fusion of genetically determined speech with culturally determined language. Implicit in this conceptual perspective is the notion that meanings attached to speech signals are arbitrary, conventionally ascribed to, and learned through repeated exposure to dominant patterns of semanticity existing in the culture in which you have been immersed since birth. In a sense, your culture preserves itself predominantly through the conventional use of speech signals. In early childhood your behavior was regulated primarily by means of speech signals produced by significant others on whom you depended for your comfort and your existence. You gradually acquired the capacity to employ speech signals *intrapersonally* to regulate your behavior and to form shape, pattern, and order out of the infinite number of environmental stimuli impinging on you. We have already alluded to the seminal works of scholars such as Vygotsky and Piaget, who described developmental processes by which conventional uses of speech signals are internalized to form the bases for lifelong patterns of thought and behavior. We grant that forms of thinking may be identified which do not appear to rely primarily on internalized speech signals.[3] We would still, however, argue that *most* forms of thinking employ internalized speech signals. For an extension of this argument let us examine some of the more recent electromyographic investigations.[4]

8.2.1. Electromyographic investigations involve the registering of concealed muscular tensions of the speech apparatus at the moment of thinking "to oneself." These investigations, many of which have been conducted in the Soviet Union, are based on the premise that movements of the speech musculature during moments of silent thinking provide evidence of the functional link between speech and thought. Many Soviet psychologists and physiologists contend that most patterns of thinking may be legitimately viewed as special instances of "concealed speech."[5] Some of these researchers have demonstrated that measurable movements of the speech articulatory organs occur during simple moments of silent thought, such as counting to oneself from one to ten. Their investigations have disclosed that kinesthetic impulses from the speech organs occur in individual "sparks" or "groups of sparks" precisely corresponding to even very small moments of silent thought. The first part of our argument, therefore, concerning the role of speech in intrapersonal communication is that speech communication, whether overt or covert, is functionally related to the occurrence of intrapersonal communication.

8.2.2. Our second argument is simply this: Raising speech communication to an overt level allows us to engage in more effective intrapersonal communication. By this we mean that if we vocalize our thoughts, they are likely to be sharper, more "systematic," and easier for us to follow. Gagné and Smith discovered that when 14- to 15-year-old boys were required to "verbalize"—that is, to think out loud to themselves—during a specific problem-solving task, their performance was superior to that of boys who did not

[3] See Rudolf Arnheim, *Visual Thinking* (London: Faber and Faber Limited, 1969).

[4] Electromyographic investigations were conducted in the United States in the early 1930s. More recently, however, Soviet psychologists and physiologists have refined and updated this line of research. See, for example, "Electromyographic Investigations," in *Psychological Science in the USSR*, Vol. I (Washington, D. C.: U. S. Joint Publications Research Service, 1961), pp. 683–700.

[5] "Electromyographic Investigations," p. 683.

verbalize during the problem-solving task.[6] Perhaps more to the point, however, is a series of studies conducted on problem-solving processes employed by college students whose tasks involved more complicated "reasoning" problems.[7] Our particular interest in these studies is that the college students were induced to verbalize as they solved the problems. Consequently, we are able to draw some general distinctions between the kinds of intrapersonal speech communication patterns which distinguished the successful from the unsuccessful problem solvers. Table 8.1 represents our inferences from this research.[8]

An additional observation grows out of this research. After having given up on some of the problems, nonsuccessful individuals were persuaded to attempt very systematically and doggedly to solve the problems. Many were able to do so. While successful problem solving may depend, at least partially, on adequate levels of knowledge and skill, we might suggest that successful problem solving is also partially determined by the forms that intrapersonal speech communication takes during problem-solving attempts.

8.2.3. One of the distinguishing features of intrapersonal speech communication, alluded to in Barker and Wiseman's general model, is that the individual relies on himself for evaluation and/or correction of his communication outcomes. In interpersonal and person-to-persons speech communication, there are external sources of evaluation, revision, and correction, but in intrapersonal speech communication the individual is at his own mercy. Suppose you tell yourself that people are basically untrustworthy. You may reflect on this formulation, interpret your experiences in a very idiosyncratic way, and then confirm your original formulation. Your behavior in subsequent interpersonal or person-to-persons communication encounters will probably be affected by your original formulation that "people are not to be trusted." However, it is doubtful that interpersonal or person-to-persons communication encounters will

[6] Robert M. Gagné and Ernest C. Smith, Jr., "A Study of the Effects of Verbalization on Problem Solving," *Journal of Experimental Psychology*, 63 (1962), 12–18.

[7] These studies are collected and reprinted in Chapter 2, "Reasoning," in Theodore L. Harris and Wilson E. Schwahn, eds., *Selected Readings on The Learning Process* (New York: Oxford University Press, 1961), pp. 31–79.

[8] For this summary we have relied heavily on Benjamin S. Bloom and Lois J. Broder, "Problem-Solving Processes of College Students," in Harris and Schwahn, *op. cit.*, pp. 59–79.

TABLE 8.1   SOME DIFFERENCES BETWEEN HIGH- AND
LOW-SUCCESS PROBLEM SOLVERS

High success	*Low success*
1. Starting the attack on the problem	
Able to select some phrase or concept as a point of departure. Able to state a specific objective toward which to work.	Tried to change the problem to one which they could solve more easily. Tendency to disagree with the problem, for example, "This is a stupid problem."
2. Approach to basic ideas within the problem	
Used analogies and examples to help themselves understand the concepts within the problems. Considered more implications of the ideas which they came up with, such as, "What would result from . . ." "What causes. . . ."	Did not attempt to arrive at an understanding of the problem, for example, "We haven't studied that yet." Used more unconnected series of thoughts.
3. General approach to problems	
Set up hypotheses about what the correct answer would do. If unfamiliar terms were used in the problem, made an assumption about the meaning and proceeded.	Selected answers on the basis of feeling and impressions (especially in social problems). Devoted little time to considering the nature of the problem.
4. Attitudes toward solving problems	
"You can figure it out if you try."	"You either know it or you don't." Easily discouraged. Avoided complex problems. Little confidence in their own reasoning abilities.

result in a correction of your original formulation. In fact, people who try to act trustworthy may simply provide you with additional evidence that people are capable of being very devious. Because of the ease with which we can confirm or validate our own conclusions, it is important that we examine the nature of our intrapersonal speech communication processes. The next two sections of this chapter present some general perspectives from which to view some of the more stable patterns of intrapersonal speech communication.

8.3. Life Orientation and Assigning Meaning. The model we began with emphasized the interactions between life orientations and the reception and transmission of messages. Many conceptual frameworks have been advanced to describe life orientations, life styles, preferences for ways to live, and so on. We are particularly interested in the conceptual framework advanced by Charles Morris, because Morris's work includes a specific concern for the influence of life orientations on the ways in which people assign meaning and the ways in which they talk about their perceptions.[9] Morris had individuals in the United States, Canada, Norway, China, India, and Japan rate 13 possible ways to live on a like–dislike scale. Subsequent analyses showed that in the United States and India five basic dimensions described individual preferences for ways to live. These five basic dimensions follow.

Factor A: Social Restraint and Self-Control. The stress here is on responsible, conscientious, intelligent participation in human affairs. The orientation is primarily moral, with an awareness of the larger human and cosmic setting in which the individual lives and an acceptance of the restraints required by responsibility to this larger whole. The accent is on the appreciation and conservation of what man has attained rather than on the initiation of change. The antithesis of this factor is unrestrained and socially irresponsible enjoyment.

Factor B: Enjoyment and Progress in Action. In this case, the stress is on delight in vigorous action to overcome obstacles. The emphasis is on the initiation of change rather than on the preservation of what has already been attained. The temper is one of confidence in man's powers rather than one of caution and restraint. The orientation is outward to society and to nature. The antithesis of the factor is a life focused on the development of the inner self.

Factor C: Withdrawal and Self-Sufficiency. A rich inner life of heightened self-awareness is stressed. The self rather than society is the focus of attention. The emphasis is not on self-indulgence, however, but rather on the simplification and purification of the self to attain a high level of insight and awareness. Control over persons and things is repudiated, but not deep sympathy for all living things. The antithesis of the factor is merging the self with the social group for group achievement and enjoyment.

[9] Charles Morris, *Varieties of Human Value* (Chicago: University of Chicago Press, 1956); *Signification and Significance* (Cambridge, Mass.: The M.I.T. Press, 1964).

Factor D: Receptivity and Sympathetic Concern. The emphasis is on receptivity to persons and to nature. The source of inspiration comes from outside the self, and the person lives and develops in devoted responsiveness to this source. This factor is not as sharply defined as are the other factors, but a stress on responsive and devoted receptivity is clearly a mode of orientation different from that represented by any other factor.

Factor E: Self-Indulgence (or Sensuous Enjoyment). Sensuous enjoyment is stressed, whether it is found in the simple pleasures of life or in abandonment to the moment. The emphasis on social restraint and self-control characteristic of Factor *A* is rejected. The antithesis of the factor is responsible submission of oneself to social and cosmic purposes.[10]

8.4. Morris further reduced these five basic dimensions to three dimensions of value; detachment, dominance, and dependence. Dominance is related to Factor *B*. Detachment is related to Factors *A* and *C*. Dependence is related to Factors *D* and *E*. Of particular interest is Morris's analysis of relationships between these three dimensions of value and ways in which individuals adhering to these values characteristically "signify," "inquire," and talk to themselves and others.

Individuals who adhere to the detachment value tend to assign meaning to stimuli on the basis of their perception of what has happened, is happening, or will happen. When these individuals are confronted with problem situations, they adopt a form of inquiry labeled "designative." They tend to make factual statements about the matter.

Individuals who adhere to the dominance value tend to assign meaning on the basis of their perception of what should be done. When confronted with problem situations, they adopt a form of inquiry labeled "prescriptive." They tend to talk to themselves and others about courses of action, what should be done, what ought to be the case.

Individuals who adhere to the dependence value tend to assign meaning on the basis of their perception of the relative values of

---

[10] Morris, 1964, pp. 24–25.

things. When confronted with problem situations, they tend to adopt a form of inquiry labeled "appraisive." They talk to themselves and others about what is good or bad, what is preferred, what is inherently more or less valuable.

An example may help to clarify this conceptual scheme. Assume that you are caught shoplifting in a department store. An identical report of this arrest reaches three of your friends. The life orientation of one of your friends corresponds to the detachment value. This friend is likely to "signify," inquire into the situation, and make utterances about it that are designative in nature. He talks to himself in the following manner: "So-and-so was busted for shoplifting. I wonder if it's true. Maybe there was some misunderstanding. If he did it, I wonder what he was trying to lift at the time. What would have made him do it? Next time I see him I'm going to find out what happened." A second friend has a life orientation corresponding to the dominance value. He is likely to "signify," inquire, and make utterances that are prescriptive in nature. He talks to himself in the following manner: "What do you do when something like that happens? Probably the best thing is to try to keep your record clean and to get the charge lifted. He'd better get himself a lawyer. Maybe he can get it cleaned up without letting his folks know about it. He'd better work out some explanation that will get him off the hook. Next time I see him I'm going to ask him how he handled it." The third friend has a life orientation corresponding to the dependence value. He is likely to "signify," inquire, and make utterances which are appraisive in nature. He talks to himself in the following manner: "What a stupid thing to do. I thought he had more sense than that. At least I figured he was smart enough not to get caught. Could he possibly have thought that what he was doing was all right? Next time I see him I'm going to tell him what a dumb ass he was."

The example, at least so far as it applies to you, may be inappropriate. But we think it illustrates the different forms which intrapersonal speech communication might be expected to take, depending on the life orientation of a given communicator. As we have indicated several times, the forms taken by intrapersonal speech communication will form the bases for that which will occur in interpersonal and frequently in person-to-persons communication. How we talk to ourselves about a phenomenon has at least partial implication for the way we talk with others about it.

8.5. Feedback and the Nature of Beliefs. One of the more critical distinctions between intrapersonal and other forms of speech communication involves the ease with which intrapersonal speech communication may be employed to perpetuate certain types of beliefs. The model from which we developed our discussion of intrapersonal speech communication identified two feedback channels, internal and external, both of which deal with self-feedback. The external channel refers to instances in which we hear ourselves talk. The internal channel refers to instances in which we attend to our "thinking." We have argued that the internal channel represents instances of "inner" or "concealed" speech.

8.5.1. The basic distinction between intrapersonal and other forms of speech communication is that intrapersonal speech communication is less likely to result in change. For example, I may gradually formulate the conclusion, based on my idiosyncratic interpretation of my experiences, that people are basically untrustworthy. If I vocalize the conclusion it sounds reasonable to me. If I reflect on it, it still seems reasonable. Indeed, even if I convince myself that I should "test" the conclusion by systematically reviewing the evidence I have for or against it, I am not likely to talk myself out of it. I may even convince myself that I have given the conclusion a fair test and that, as a matter of fact, I have shrewdly discerned something which others have frequently been incapable of realizing. In short, I have weighed the facts and have found that I was right, as I suspected all along.

To inquire further into the nature of intrapersonal speech communication, let us consider types of beliefs and the different communication levels on which they are primarily formed and maintained. The perspective we have adopted comes from the work of Rokeach, specifically his explanation of five basic types of beliefs.[11]

1. Type A: Primitive Beliefs, 100% Consensus, are formed from a person's early experiences with the object of belief. The object of belief may be some aspect of physical reality, social reality, or the nature of the self. The distinguishing characteristic of primitive beliefs is that they are based on and maintained through social

---

[11] Milton Rokeach, *Beliefs, Attitudes and Values* (San Francisco: Jossey-Bass, Inc., Publishers, 1968).

consensus. I am a man, and everyone I know can be expected to reinforce my belief that I am a man. I know my name, and everyone else who is in a position to know me by name will agree that I am who I claim to be. My occupational category is "teacher," a fact about which I have never encountered, nor would I ever expect to encounter, any disagreement. I also have a belief about my competence as a teacher, but I would not expect 100% consensus concerning that belief, since it is not a primitive belief of Type *A*. We could continue to enumerate my Type *A* primitive beliefs, listing statements about physical reality, social reality, and the nature of my "self," each statement representing something I believe to be true, that I have directly experienced, and on which I expect unanimous agreement. These beliefs are central to my system of beliefs, in the sense that many other beliefs are connected with them and also in the sense that any change in these primitive beliefs would presumably require considerable changes in other types of beliefs making up my belief system.

2. *Type B: Primitive Beliefs, 0% Consensus.* Another type of belief arises from our direct experience with the world around us but is not based on or maintained through social consensus. Some beliefs are based on our own idiosyncratic interpretation of our experiences. On these beliefs we do not expect anything approaching complete agreement on the part of others. Nevertheless, these beliefs may be so central to our view of the world that they are highly resistant to change. We may even expect to encounter some controversy with respect to these beliefs, but as Rokeach says, "Beliefs that are not shared with others are therefore impervious to persuasion or argument by others."[12] I may believe in God. I may believe that I possess an uncanny knack for distinguishing good people from bad people. I may believe that people like me only for my money. I may believe that people distrust me. I may believe that if I talk in class people will think I'm stupid. I may believe that my son is far more intelligent than other boys his age. I may believe that mankind is irreversibly headed toward self-destruction. Any or all of these beliefs may be essential to my view of the world and the people in it. Hence, many of the other beliefs that make up my belief system are influenced by, or directly connected with, these types of primitive beliefs.

[12] Rokeach, p. 8.

3. Type C: Authority Beliefs. The early emergence and stability of Type *A* primitive beliefs allows us to develop some confidence in a socially-based definition of reality. Inevitably, however, and usually early in life, we begin to experience controversy over some beliefs for which we had come to expect total agreement. Some of the beliefs we had accepted as basic truths are increasingly questioned. We are forced to make finer judgments about whom we can rely on to tell us the way things really are. So we begin to identify the positive and negative authorities and begin to invest different levels of confidence in their statements. For most of us, the first positive authorities in whom considerable confidence was invested were our parents. Gradually, however, we probably discovered that our parents, though usually reliable, did not always tell us the truth. Sometimes they helped us develop Type *A* primitive beliefs which we subsequently discovered were false. At any rate, we have come to expect differences of opinion on some of our beliefs, and we have established some rough and some very fine distinctions enabling us to decide who is likely to know and who can be trusted to be truthful about what he knows. These judgments are directed toward sources of information which may be single individuals, small groups, or very large classes of individuals.

4. Type D: Derived Beliefs. Our learned willingness to trust and rely on certain sources of information results in our acceptance of other beliefs deriving from certain sources. Indeed, most of the "facts" you have at your disposal, whether they be historical, geographical, scientific, political, or even sociological, represent things you believe to be true but have never experienced directly. Most of these beliefs are derived from sources you have assumed to be, in some ways, legitimate sources of information.

5. Type E: Inconsequential Beliefs. Inconsequential beliefs are matters of taste. Sue is more attractive than Mary. Russian salad dressing tastes better than French. One pair of pants is more fashionable than another. These beliefs are not inconsequential in the sense that they do not matter to the individual holding them. On the contrary, inconsequential beliefs may be held as rigidly, and sometimes as violently, as any other type of belief. But inconsequential beliefs are not ordinarily central to an individual's belief system. They are not ordinarily connected with a great many other beliefs. A change in an inconsequential belief does not ordinarily wreak havoc with other parts of an individual's belief system.

8.6. Let us return now to a consideration of the nature of intrapersonal speech communication. We have said that intrapersonal speech communication occurs whenever meaning or significance is attached to an internally or externally generated stimulus. We have said also that most forms of intrapersonal communication may be regarded as instances of intrapersonal speech communication which provide us with self-feedback whenever we hear ourselves talk or attend to our "inner" or "concealed" speech. It is now possible for us to identify types of beliefs which are formed and maintained primarily through intrapersonal speech communication. These beliefs are, for the most part, Type *B* primitive beliefs. Type *B* primitive beliefs depend on intrapersonal speech communication for their formation and perpetuation. This is not an absolute distinction. Other types of beliefs are influenced by intrapersonal speech communication, and Type *B* primitive beliefs may be influenced by phenomena occurring at the interpersonal and person-to-persons levels. However, the primary source for Type *B* primitive beliefs is the things we tell ourselves about our experience with the world and its inhabitants.

Consider the bases for the various belief types and what would be involved in bringing about a fundamental change of belief in each of the five types. Type *A* primitive beliefs might be extremely difficult to change; in fact, Rokeach describes these beliefs as "incontrovertible." But we would contend that Type *A* beliefs are changeable, though their change is seldom attempted. If we could control the utterances made by all the individuals with whom you come into contact, we could probably change many, if not all, of your Type *A* primitive beliefs. At the very least, you would rapidly become confused and disoriented. Similarly, we could change many of your inconsequential beliefs. In fact, many matters of personal taste are already recognized as being heavily influenced by broader social judgments, or at least judgments within an individual's peer group. If we could control the utterances of specific individuals in whom you have confidence, we could rapidly change a given one of your authority beliefs. Of course, derived beliefs are probably the most easily changed. Dramatic and consistent scientific testimony might even convince you that Jupiter has exploded and vanished from our solar system.

Now assume that you know someone who believes intensely that other individuals are motivated primarily by selfish interest and are likely to be extremely deceptive. How difficult would it be to change that belief, and what long-range, concerted program can you imagine that might reasonably be expected to bring about a change in that belief? We contend that Type *B* primitive beliefs are highly resistant to change precisely because of one of the distinguishing characteristics of intrapersonal speech communication: its heavy reliance on self-correcting mechanisms.

Individuals may differ in the extent to which their intrapersonal speech communication messages approximate some external "reality." They may differ in the extent to which their intrapersonal speech communication processes are influenced by their life orientations. Individuals may even differ in the extent to which their Type *B* primitive beliefs are held unquestioningly, or with great confidence. But most of us are probably not aware of, or not attuned to, our own intrapersonal speech communication processes. Greater awareness of and attention to these processes has been our present objective.

SUMMARY

1. Intrapersonal communication occurs whenever meaning or significance is attached to an internally or externally generated stimulus.

2. Much "thought" may be regarded as instances of "inner" or "concealed" speech communication.

3. Raising intrapersonal communication to a vocal level may sharpen and facilitate reasoning.

4. High- and low-success problem solvers differ in the patterns of intrapersonal speech communication they employ during problem-solving tasks.

5. An individual's life orientation may be expected to influence directly his characteristic patterns of intrapersonal speech communication.

6. Intrapersonal speech communication, specifically the ways in which individuals assign meaning and inquire into problem situations, may be characterized as designative, prescriptive, and appraisive.

7. One of the distinguishing characteristics of intrapersonal speech communication is its heavy reliance on self-correction and self-validation.

8. Types of beliefs may generally be distinguished in terms of the extent to which they are formed and maintained primarily through intrapersonal speech communication.

EXERCISES

1. A myth has been defined as "a belief held uncritically." In small discussion groups, individually identify a myth, popularly accepted by others, in which you do not believe. After each person has identified such a myth, discuss the various ways and mechanisms through which these myths are preserved.

2. Being as specific as possible, detail a procedure you would follow to convince someone that he is not who he thinks he is. Over what communicative conditions would you need to exercise control for your strategy to be effective?

3. Identify a Type *B* primitive belief which you currently hold. Outline the circumstances or experiences which you feel might bring you to a substantial modification of that belief.

ADDITIONAL READINGS

Borden, George A., Richard B. Gregg, and Theodore G. Grove, *Speech Behavior and Human Interaction*, Section I, "The Individual's Communication System." Englewood Cliffs, N. J.: Prentice-Hall, Inc., 1969.

Goffman, Erving, *The Presentation of Self in Everyday Life*. Garden City, N. Y.: Doubleday & Company, Inc., 1959.

Johnson, Wendell, *Your Most Enchanted Listener*. New York: Harper and Row, Publishers, 1956.

Reik, Theodor, *Voices From the Inaudible: The Patients Speak*. New York: Farrar, Straus & Giroux, Inc., 1964.

Chapter 9

THE

INTERPERSONAL

LEVEL

9.1. At this point in our discussion we may take an almost limitless number of conceptually different directions. Speech communication at the interpersonal level has been so widely and diversely analyzed, both in scholarly and popular journals and settings, that what any of us may choose to say about it seems almost to depend on our way of viewing the human condition. Some people say that we should talk with each other in ways which will allow us to become autonomous individuals. Others insist that there is great value in talking with each other in ways which are "authentic," "open," "honest," and "congruent." Some say that our communication with each other should further the development and maintenance of high levels of mutual trust. Others say that interpersonal speech communication should allow us to solve calmly and rationally problems of mutual concern. Another view is that as we talk with each other we should conduct ourselves in ways that will allow others to value themselves, to confirm their basic worth as individuals. Many people claim that interpersonal speech communication is important insofar as we can accurately send and receive messages, so that we may understand each other at least as well as we must to perform the routine cooperative chores required in almost all human collective activity. Some hold that almost all interpersonal speech communication is essentially persuasive and that we should understand the basic processes involved in influencing others and in attempts directed at influencing us.

Each of us probably has his own notions about which interpersonal outcomes are most desirable, either for improving the human condition or for accomplishing our individual goals. Similarly, each of us probably has his own repertoire of preferred interpersonal speech communication "styles." Accumulated research efforts tend to support the conclusion that our interpersonal behavior is at least as varied as the ends toward which it is directed. A recent study reported by Beisecker illustrates this point.[1] Beisecker investigated the speech communication behavior of 40 individuals interacting in pairs, for up to 30 minutes, on two "potentially controversial topics": mass protest and university control over nonacademic affairs of undergraduate students. Beisecker warns that his investigation is limited in a number of ways; nevertheless, this tentative exploration resulted in the identification of some basically different "orientations" characterizing the participants. Interpersonal speech communication patterns varied with the topic of discussion. Some of the more clearly discernible patterns were (1) "states and defends position on issue," characterized by the initiation, amplification, and substantiation of certain ideas, the rejection of other ideas, and the modification of previously presented ideas; (2) "avoids influencing or probing the position of the other," characterized by favorable modifications of previously presented ideas, avoidance of rejecting ideas, and avoidance of questions dealing with the issue at hand; (3) "structures interpersonal relations," characterized by communication directed toward the nature of the interpersonal relationship; and (4) "withdraws," characterized by the relative absence of communication directed toward the nature of the interpersonal relationship, relative absence of initiating new ideas, and some tendency to reject new ideas introduced.

[1] Thomas D. Beisecker, "Communication Strategies in Interpersonal Interactions: A Factor Analysis Study" (paper presented at the International Communication Association Annual Conference, Phoenix, Arizona, April 1971).

Many other interpersonal styles or patterns can be elaborated.[2] However, we cannot hope in this chapter to do justice to the wide variety of goals, strategies, and patterns represented in the multifaceted phenomenon that is our present focus. We intend here to discuss some selected aspects of interpersonal speech communication. We have arbitrarily focused our attention on those aspects which, in our experience, have been of interest and concern to our students. The list of additional readings at the end of this chapter will lead you to material encompassing additional interests and concerns.

9.2. Confirming and Disconfirming Responses. Over the past decade has come a kind of mass movement of attitudes, increasingly discernible and audible, suggesting to us in a variety of ways that no matter what other goals or strategies surround our communication with others, we should behave toward others in ways likely at least to improve the quality of interpersonal relationships. The preface to *Interpersonal Dynamics* contains the following statements:

> . . . national and international conflagrations have their counterparts at every level of human intercourse: in small groups, in marriages, in friendships, among lovers and siblings, between teachers and students, between worker and boss. Unless the protagonists are famous, the tensions go unnoticed, to be registered indirectly and anonymously in divorce rates, homicides, and gang wars or often in the more pedestrian way civilized people live with their human problems: poison pen letters, petty jealousies, unproductive relationships, prejudices, practical jokes, destructive fantasies, unstable careers, ulcerative colitis, frayed nerves, tranquilizers, and sleeping pills.[3]

We do not purport to have the solution to all interpersonal problems, but we wish to examine with a few exploratory probes some concepts which may prove useful in understanding speech communication behaviors related to the general quality of human interaction. Our concern follows Barnlund's focus on constructive

[2] For a discussion of some styles or patterns which seem to have considerable impact on interpersonal outcomes, see Chapter 7, "General Response Tendencies," in James McCroskey, Carl Larson, and Mark Knapp, *An Introduction to Interpersonal Communication* (Englewood Cliffs, N. J.: Prentice-Hall, Inc., 1971).

[3] Warren G. Bennis, Edgar H. Schein, David E. Berlew, and Fred I. Steele, *Interpersonal Dynamics* (Homewood, Ill.: Dorsey Press, 1964), p. ix.

communicative relationships,[4] and Watzlawick, Beavin, and Jackson's focus on the nature of "healthy" communicative patterns.[5] Our specific perspective is that of Sieburg, who distinguishes between *confirming* and *disconfirming* responses in the speech communication behavior of individuals.[6] In interaction between persons *A* and *B*, confirming responses occur whenever person *B* responds to person *A*'s communicative attempt in a way that causes *A* to value himself more. Disconfirming responses occur when *B*'s responses to *A*'s communicative attempts cause *A* to value himself less.

Sieburg's comprehensive review of theoretical and clinical literature related to the qualities of human interaction, analyses of "live" interaction in group and interpersonal contacts, and subsequent refinement of her conclusions through a survey of members of the International Communication Association led to the identification of twelve basic categories of confirming and disconfirming responses. Seven of the categories described disconfirming responses, and five categories described confirming responses.

9.2.1. Disconfirming responses

1. *Impervious response.* When one speaker fails to acknowledge, even minimally, the other speaker's communicative attempt, or when one ignores or disregards the other by not giving any ostensible acknowledgement of the other's communication, his response may be called impervious.

2. *Interrupting response.* When one speaker cuts the other speaker short or begins while the other is still speaking, his response may be called interrupting.

3. *Irrelevant response.* When one speaker responds in a way that seems unrelated to what the other has been saying, or when one speaker introduces a new topic without warning or returns to his earlier topic, apparently disregarding the intervening conversation, his response may be called irrelevent.

---

[4] Dean C. Barnlund, *Interpersonal Communication: Survey and Studies* (Boston: Houghton Mifflin Company, 1968).

[5] Paul Watzlawick, Janet Beavin, and Don Jackson, *Pragmatics of Human Communication* (New York: W. W. Norton & Co., Inc., 1967).

[6] Evelyn Sieburg, "Dysfunctional Communication and Interpersonal Responsiveness in Small Groups" (unpublished dissertation, University of Denver, 1969); Evelyn Sieburg and Carl Larson, "Dimensions of Interpersonal Response" (paper presented at the International Communication Association Annual Conference, Phoenix, Arizona, April 1971).

4. *Tangential response.* When one speaker acknowledges the other person's communication but immediately takes the conversation in another direction, his response may be called tangential. Occasionally, individuals exhibit what may appear to be direct responses to the other, such as "Yes, but . . ." or "Well, you may be right, but . . .," but then may proceed to respond with communicative content very different from or unrelated to that which preceded. Such responses may still be called tangential.

5. *Impersonal response.* When a speaker conducts a monologue, when his speech communication behavior appears intellectualized, impersonal, containing few first-person statements and more generalized "you" or "one" statements and is heavily loaded with euphemisms or clichés, the response may be called impersonal.

6. *Incoherent response.* When the speaker responds with sentences that are incomplete or with rambling statements difficult to follow, containing much retracing or rephrasing, or interjections such as "you know" or "I mean," his response may be called incoherent.

7. *Incongruous response.* When the speaker engages in nonvocal behavior that seems inconsistent with the vocal content, his response may be called incongruous. For example, "Who's angry? I'm not angry!" (said in a tone and volume that strongly suggests anger). Or, "I'm really concerned about you" (said in a tone that suggests lack of interest or disdain).

The total impact of such responses, or combinations of them, is to cause another person to value himself less. Disconfirming responses imply that the other person's communicative attempts do not warrant direct acknowledgement or serious attention. A highly disconfirming individual seems to be saying not only "You are not worth considering seriously," but almost appears to be saying, "You do not exist."

9.2.2. Confirming responses

1. *Direct acknowledgment.* One speaker acknowledges the other's communication and reacts to it directly and verbally.

2. *Agreement about content.* One speaker reinforces or supports information or opinions expressed by the other.

3. *Supportive response.* One speaker expresses understanding of the other, reassures him, or tries to make him feel better.

4. *Clarifying response.* One speaker tries to clarify the content of the other's message or attempts to clarify the other's present or past feelings. The usual form of a clarifying response is to elicit more

information, to encourage the other to say more, or to repeat in an inquiring way what was understood.

5. *Expression of positive feeling.* One speaker describes his own positive feelings related to prior utterances of the other; for example, "Okay, now I understand what you are saying."

Confirming and disconfirming responses provide us with a conceptual point of departure for attacking the complicated questions related to the nature of speech communication transactions which are likely to lead to mutually adaptive, functional relationships. There is a common thread running through reports of individuals' speech communication interactions which have resulted in feelings of alienation, interpersonal antagonism, and even mild forms of personal despair, which is captured in the following statement, heard in many variations: "When I was talking to him I got the impression that what I had to say really didn't matter."

9.3. Interpersonal Attraction. The confirming and disconfirming aspects of interpersonal speech communication tend to lead us to value ourselves more or less. A conceptually related set of questions has to do with those aspects of speech communication which lead us to value *others* more or less. As we shall see, there are very definite relationships between those speech communication phenomena which tend to result in higher valuations of self and those which tend to result in higher valuations of others. A general framework through which we may explore these relationships is represented in Figure 9.1.[7]

	Initial phases	*Intermediate phases*	*Subsequent phases*
Foundations for attraction	Properties of people Physical attractiveness	Social rewards Reinforcement	Interpersonal similarity Evaluative orientations
Sources of the foundations	Personal tastes and values	Orientations toward self	Orientations toward objects of discussion
Important communication variables	Perception of object characteristics Judger's priorities	Nature of feedback Self-opinion and perception of evaluator	Perception of people characteristics Degrees of disclosure and importance of topics

FIGURE 9.1 Tentative notions about interpersonal attraction phases.

[7] McCroskey, Larson, and Knapp, p. 49.

Figure 9.1 is based on the assumption that various types of information related to our perceptions of others will be relatively more visible or discernible during different phases of our encounters with others. Let us consider the phases separately.

9.3.1. Initial phases. Ordinarily, the information which is immediately available to us in the early phases of our encounter with another is that which allows us to make judgments about the physical properties of the other. We do not suggest that physical properties are the only important determinants of interpersonal attraction in its initial phases, but we do suggest that in the initial phases interpersonal attraction depends more heavily on judgments we make about the properties of people we encounter. There is evidence of our considerable agreement and consistency in judging the physical attractiveness of others.[8] An interesting line of research is followed by investigators who randomly pair couples for "computer dances." In one investigation, after gathering a battery of personality, intellectual, and scholastic aptitude measures, the researchers attempted to predict which individuals would be liked best, whether a person would want to date his partner again, and whether a person would actually ask his partner for another date. In this instance the researchers discovered that the only good predictor of one person's attraction to another was the other's physical attractiveness.[9] In another investigation, physical attractiveness, the other's sociability, and the other's perceived similar interests were found to be correlated with desire to date again.[10] In a somewhat related study researchers found that interpersonal attraction was greater toward physically attractive strangers regardless of whether the strangers were of the same or opposite sex.[11]

Recently there has emerged an implied desire on the part of some groups, especially some student subcultures, to deemphasize eval-

[8] Peter B. Warr and Christopher Knapper, *The Perception of People and Events* (New York: John Wiley & Sons, Inc., 1968); A. H. Iliffe, "A Study of Preferences in Feminine Beauty," *British Journal of Psychology*, 51 (1960), 267–73.

[9] E. Walster, V. Aronson, D. Abrahams, and L. Rottman, "Importance of Physical Attractions in Dating Behavior," *Journal of Personality and Social Psychology*, 4 (1966), 508–16.

[10] R. W. Brislin and S. A. Lewis, "Dating and Physical Attractiveness," *Psychological Reports*, 22 (1968), 976 *et passim*.

[11] D. Byrne, O. London, and K. Reeves, "The Effects of Physical Attractiveness, Sex, and Attitude Similarity on Interpersonal Attraction," *Journal of Personality*, 36 (1968), 259–71.

uative judgments based on properties of people. Nevertheless, it seems to us that these subcultures have adopted manners of dress and demeanor which carry informational value on which interpersonal judgments are based, especially within a given subculture. Consequently, although the personal tastes and values of the evaluator may change from generation to generation, or from group to group, it still seems reasonable to conclude that in the initial phases of interpersonal encounters individuals continue to base interpersonal judgments on physical properties of others.

9.3.2. Social rewards. In the intermediate phases of interpersonal encounters we see some links between speech communication processes related to valuation of self and those processes related to valuation of others. However, there are specific exceptions to the general conclusion that we tend to value those who confirm us and devalue those who disconfirm us. One exception has to do with the sincerity, or lack of sincerity, of the other's responses to us. Iverson reports the results of an investigation concluding that we tend to dislike those who offer "phony" flattery; however, if such apparently insincere responses come from higher-status others, we are still inclined to respond favorably.[12]

That we tend to be attracted toward those who praise us, confirm us, or provide us with social rewards may not seem surprising. There is, however, another interesting exception to this general conclusion. A question that has been raised in the literature on interpersonal attraction concerns the extent to which individuals who have low opinions of themselves will respond favorably to positive evaluations. One theory suggests that individuals respond positively to those who provide positive evaluation, regardless of whether the individuals have positive or negative self-concepts. A different theoretical argument suggests that individuals will respond positively to evaluations that are consistent with their own self-concept. Thus, individuals with low self-opinion would be expected to react favorably to negative evaluations. In an investigation directed toward answering some of these questions, Jones and Schneider discovered that a mediating variable exists: individuals who are relatively certain that their low self-opinions are legitimate respond favorably to the negative evaluator, and individuals who are

[12] M. A. Iverson, "Attraction Toward Flatterers of Different Statuses," *Journal of Social Psychology*, 74 (1968), 181–87.

relatively uncertain of the legitimacy of their low self-opinions respond favorably to the positive evaluator.[13] Consequently, there are at least some tentative reasons to believe that positively evaluative responses from others are not universally favored.

9.3.3. Interpersonal similarity.   Information concerning the extent to which individuals exhibit similarities to us or share similar attitudes, beliefs, and values is likely to emerge in subsequent phases of interpersonal encounters. Research on the relationships between interpersonal similarity and attraction supports the notion that the two phenomena are complementary. That is, individuals with similar attitudes tend to become more highly attracted to each other over time, and individuals who are mutually attracted and who interact with each other tend to develop more similar attitudes.[14] Thus, elements of confirmation appear important in subsequent phases of interpersonal encounter to the extent that we are more attracted to individuals whose evaluative orientations toward the objects of discussion are similar to our own.

Of course, many other bases may undergird the formation and maintenance of interpersonal attraction. Each of us would probably claim considerable uniqueness in how he evaluates others and the bases on which he accepts or rejects them. Nevertheless, it is probably an exceptionally tolerant and thick-skinned person who continues to interact with another, unless forced to, in the presence of disconfirming responses, implied or expressed negative evaluations, and in the absence of some minimal level of support for his own attitudes, values, and beliefs.

9.4. Accuracy of Interpersonal Judgments. For many years one of the principal outcomes focused on in the study of interpersonal communication was accuracy in the transmission, reception, and decoding of messages. A dominant concern was whether one person understood what another said. Concern for this outcome is still

[13] S. C. Jones and D. J. Schneider, "Certainty of Self-Appraisal and Reactions to Evaluations from Others," *Sociometry*, 31 (1968), 395–403.

[14] See, for example, H. F. Taylor, "Balance and Change in the Two-Person Group," *Sociometry*, 30 (1967), 262–79; G. L. Clore and B. Baldridge, "Interpersonal Attraction: The Role of Agreement and Topic Interest," *Journal of Personality and Social Psychology*, 9 (1968), 340–46; R. E. Brewer, "Attitude Change, Interpersonal Attraction, and Communication in a Dyadic Situation," *Journal of Social Psychology*, 75 (1968), 127–34.

strong, as indeed it probably always legitimately will be. Nevertheless, we have seen a growing concern for a corollary type of understanding that involves one person's ability to understand another as a person, to identify accurately the other person's attitudes, values, beliefs, preferences, sentiments, and feelings—one person's ability to adopt the point of view of the other, to view people, events, and circumstances in ways which at least approximate the ways in which the other views these phenomena. Many labels have been invented to describe this ability: person perception, interpersonal perception, sensitivity, social perception, empathic ability, awareness, empathy, judging accuracy, and so on. As a systematic and concerted research focus, it is of relatively recent origin. Still, it has considerable intuitive appeal because conceptually it seems to encompass many of the concerns of people actively working for the improvement of interpersonal communication. We will arbitrarily call this variable "empathic ability" because there is some evidence that it is an ability, or trait, characterizing individuals in varying degrees.[15]

You may be used to thinking of empathic ability in terms of phrases such as "good judge of character," "very sensitive person," or "really understands human nature." Concepts such as these are difficult to assess in carefully controlled research studies. Consequently, researchers usually assess empathic ability by having one person predict how another person will describe himself, how another person will behave, or what another person's attitudes or views are. The process by which one person makes these kinds of predictions with respect to another is very complicated. The ability to make accurate interpersonal judgments is so complex that measures of empathic ability have been said to have at least 20 operational components.[16] For many years social and behavioral scientists have argued the merits of various procedures for assessing empathic ability; only recently have procedures been developed which promise to solve some of the methodological problems confronting those who wish to study it.[17]

[15] Victor B. Cline and J. M. Richards, "Accuracy of Interpersonal Perception—A General Trait?" *Journal of Abnormal and Social Psychology*, 60 (1960), 1–7.

[16] Gerald Marwell, "Problems of Operational Definitions of 'Empathy,' 'Identification,' and Related Concepts," *Journal of Social Psychology*, 63 (1964), 89–102.

[17] C. W. Hobart and Nancy Fahlberg, "The Measurement of Empathy," *American Journal of Sociology*, 70 (1965), 595–603.

9.4.1. At least two types of judging accuracy can be distinguished.[18] The first, *stereotyped accuracy*, implies a global judgment based on sensitivity to social norms and a resultant ability to predict typical or average responses for a wide range of people. For example, if I could accurately predict how a university faculty will vote on a particular issue, I would presumably be accurate by virtue of a well defined and generally accurate stereotype of university faculty members. The second type of judging accuracy, *differential accuracy*, implies a more analytical judgment based on sensitivity to differences between persons. For example, if I could accurately predict how individual faculty members in my department will vote, such accuracy presumably would require more refined judgments, taking into account differences between, rather than similarities among, those I am judging. It is important to remember that both of these forms of judging may, in particular instances, produce accurate judgments.

9.4.2. The distinction between stereotyped and differential accuracy leads in two directions, with some inevitable conceptual confusion. One direction leads us to Gage's early experiments in which college and high school students attempted to predict college student responses on a self-description inventory.[19] Some of the students were asked to make their predictions only on the basis of their knowledge that they were judging a "typical male undergraduate in teacher training at the University of Illinois." Other students observed the targets of their judgments and then made their predictions. In two similar studies Gage found that the students whose predictions were based on stereotypes were more accurate in their judgments than those students making post-observation predictions. In a later experiment two investigators asked judges to identify deception attempts made by an interviewee.[20] Some of the judges watched and heard the interview, some only listened to a tape recording, and some only read a transcript of the interview. Those who listened to the recording or read the transcript were more accurate in their identification of deception attempts than were

[18] Cline and Richards, *op. cit.*

[19] N. L. Gage, "Judging Interests from Expressive Behavior," *Psychological Monographs*, 65, No. 18, (1952).

[20] N. R. Maier and J. A. Thurber, "Accuracy of Judgments of Deception When an Interview Is Watched, Heard, and Read," *Personnel Psychology*, 21 (1968), 23–30.

those who watched and heard the interview. In academic discussions of empathic ability this experiment is sometimes used to support the contention that global judgments are frequently more accurate than analytical judgments precisely because, in any interpersonal encounter, so many irrelevant and extraneous cues are provided that an individual who relies predominantly on analytical judgments is frequently led astray. If you will recall our earlier distinction between intentional and unintentional communication, you will better appreciate that many forms of expressive behavior may occur during interpersonal communication. "Signs" or "cues" may trigger intrapersonal messages which do not necessarily correspond to the "real" messages being sent by the other. Indeed, the ease with which individuals may be misled by extraneous cues partially accounts for the continued success of the con man and is frequently relied on in political campaigns.

The observations that global judgments are occasionally more accurate than analytical judgments and that stereotyped accuracy must be considered at least a part of empathic ability are reasonable if one takes into account Campbell's analysis of stereotypes. [21] Campbell suggests that where group differences exist, they will tend to appear in the stereotypes groups have of one another. The relative accuracy of stereotypes might help to explain the results of some investigations which, taken collectively, provide evidence that interpersonal communication is effective in facilitating "understanding" (in the judging accuracy sense) if we are interacting with individuals who have similar interests, attitudes, or characteristics, but that communication may not necessarily facilitate understanding if we are interacting with others who have dissimilar interests, attitudes, or characteristics. [22]

9.4.3. Now let us follow the other direction implied by our distinction between stereotyped and differential accuracy. Remember that much of the early research on empathic ability employed rather crude assessments of the variable. Early measures

[21] D. T. Campbell, "Stereotypes and the Perception of Group Differences," *American Psychologist*, 22 (1967), 817–29.
[22] G. D. Mellinger, "Interpersonal Trust as a Factor in Communication," *Journal of Abnormal and Social Psychology*, 52 (1956), 304–9; M. M. Wilkins, "A Study of the Conditions Which Influence the Accuracy of Interpersonal Perception" (Ph.D. dissertation, University of Colorado, 1965); R. E. Brewer and M. B. Brewer, "Attraction and Accuracy of Perception in Dyads," *Journal of Personality and Social Psychology*, 8 (1968), 188–93.

probably did not adequately take into account differential accuracy. Nevertheless, a second set of research conclusions supports notions much more in line with our expectations about characteristics of accurate judges. Cline found good judges to be characterized by the absence of ethnocentric and authoritarian attitudes, the presence of superior intellectual ability, and a tendency to describe themselves as "sympathetic" and "affectionate." Poor judges describe themselves as "dissatisfied," "irritable," "awkward," "praising," and "hurried."[23] Other investigators have found that individuals who are more accurate judges tend to inquire more into the thoughts and feelings of others,[24] that more "empathic" industrial supervisors are more "considerate" toward their subordinates.[25]

9.4.4. Although both forms of judgment, global and analytical, may lead to more accurate judgments of others, they may be tentatively distinguished on the basis of the extent to which the two forms of judgment rely on specific instances of interpersonal speech communication feedback. Global judgments, for example, seem to derive their accuracy from the judger's sensitivity to social norms and greater commitment to a conventional picture of man. A conventional picture of man may, on the average, be correct, and a fine sensitivity to social norms would probably equip an individual to predict the ways in which most people will behave most of the time. Indeed, it may be argued that an "average" person can accurately judge many other people simply by assuming that the others are like him. If he assumes that others have similar attitudes, values, beliefs, and ways of behaving, then the fact that he is "average" will make his predictions correct most of the time. Consequently, global or stereotyped judgments may be accurate with comparatively little interpersonal feedback. On the other hand, the minimal requirement for differential accuracy is that an individual be capable of judging ways in which others are different from him and different from each other. Differential accuracy implies greater attention to instances of

[23] V. B. Cline, "Ability to Judge Personality Assessed with a Stress Interview and Sound-Film Technique," *Journal of Abnormal and Social Psychology*, 55 (1955), 183–87.

[24] L. W. Cooper, "The Relationship of Empathy to Aspects of Cognitive Control" (Ph.D. dissertation, Yale University, 1967).

[25] E. A. Fleishman and J. A. Salter, "Relation Between the Leader's Behavior and His Empathy Toward Subordinates," *Journal of Industrial Psychology*, 1 (1963), 79–84.

feedback provided in individual interpersonal encounters.

9.4.5. Specific attention to variations in the interpersonal communication behavior of others will probably improve the accuracy of interpersonal judgments for several reasons. (1) Earlier we contended that there is considerable interdependence among the levels on which communication occurs. A person's attitudes, values, beliefs, preferences—that is, the way an individual talks to himself about the outside world—will necessarily exercise some influence on how he talks with others. In the preceding chapter we attempted to demonstrate how important the life orientation aspect of the intrapersonal communication model is, and how an individual's speech communication behavior is influenced by this aspect. So an individual's speech communication behavior is likely to be a rich source of information regarding his inner state. (2) Having earlier argued that there is great interdependence between speech communication behavior and many forms of thinking, we might put forth the speculative assertion, certain to be challenged by many communication theorists, that speech communication behavior is more likely to correspond to an individual's "thoughts" than are most other forms of behavior, particularly expressive behavior. Of two studies cited earlier, one found that judgments based on expressive behavior were less accurate than judgments based on simple stereotypes, and another found that judges who attended to interview transcripts and tape recordings (what was said) were more accurate than judges who watched and heard the target of their judgments. Again, we are making a speculative assertion. Even though our present focus is on understanding the other person as a person, we might still achieve greater understanding by attending to the other's speech communication behavior more than to the way the person looks, how he stands, his gestures, facial expressions, and so on.

There are many other outcomes and aspects of interpersonal speech communication. The additional readings at the end of this chapter are designed to lead you to some of them. Our arbitrary focus on certain aspects of interpersonal speech communication results from recent experiences in which students expressed concern for three things: (1) those which contribute to a person's valuation of himself, (2) those which contribute to people's valuations of each other, and (3) those which are related to our understanding of one another as persons.

SUMMARY

1. Communication at the interpersonal level may be characterized in terms of a wide variety of desirable outcomes and many varied speech communication patterns and styles.

2. Confirmation and disconfirmation are concepts referring to the extent to which one person's responses to another's communicative acts result in the other's valuing himself more or less.

3. The categories of disconfirming behavior suggest an overall pattern in which responses are essentially unrelated to communication content which preceded them, and in which the responses reflect insufficient attention to or concern for what the other person is saying.

4. Categories of confirming responses suggest an overall pattern reflecting more direct response to, support for, and genuine interest in what the other person is saying.

5. Interpersonal attraction may be viewed as emerging and being maintained in three general phases of interpersonal encounters.

6. Physical attractiveness, social rewards, and interpersonal similarity seem to account for much of the basis for interpersonal attraction.

7. Interpersonal judgment may be conceptualized as global and/or analytical.

8. Both global and analytical interpersonal judgments may be accurate.

9. Analytical judgments seemed to rely more heavily on specific instances of interpersonal speech communication feedback than do global judgments.

EXERCISES

1. In groups of ten to twelve members each, discuss a topic on which there is likely to be some difference of opinion among the group members. Phrase the question initially so that the respondents may indicate their opinions with a "yes" or "no" answer. Discuss the topic for 20 to 30 minutes. At the end of the discussion ask each participant to indicate on a piece of paper his position on the issue. Ask each member also to identify his predictions of each other participant's answer. Tabulate the results on the board. Then identify the individuals who were relatively accurate in predicting other people's positions.

Also identify individuals whose answers others tended to predict accurately. Discuss and attempt to explain the results.

2. Assign several individuals the task of securing a tape recording of 20 to 30 minutes of interpersonal interaction in any particular social context (for example, a job interview, an appraisal interview). Play the tape in class, stopping it at frequent intervals to have each person attempt to categorize interpersonal responses into specific confirming and disconfirming categories. Identify and discuss the nature of those responses on which the coders have difficulty agreeing.

3. Identify the three criteria you consider the most important in determining whether you tend to like or dislike another. In groups of five to six members, compare the criteria that have been identified. Select from the total list of criteria those which you feel provide the most accurate bases for understanding another person as a person.

ADDITIONAL READINGS

Barnlund, Dean C., *Interpersonal Communication: Survey and Studies.* Boston: Houghton Mifflin Company, 1968.

Giffin, Kim, and Bobby Patton, *Fundamentals of Interpersonal Communication.* New York: Harper and Row, Publishers, 1971.

Keltner, John W., *Interpersonal Speech Communication: Elements and Structure.* Belmont, Calif.: Wadsworth Publishing Co., Inc., 1970.

McCroskey, James, Carl Larson, and Mark Knapp, *An Introduction to Interpersonal Communication.* Englewood Cliffs, N. J.: Prentice-Hall, Inc., 1971.

Giffin, Kim, "Social Alienation by Communication Denial," *Quarterly Journal of Speech*, 56 (1970), 347–57.

Chapter 10

THE

PERSON-TO-PERSONS

LEVEL

10.1. On first consideration, person-to-persons speech communication may seem to differ from the other levels of speech communication primarily along a quantitative dimension. *Intrapersonal speech communication* is a term we have used to refer to what occurs when an individual talks with himself. *Interpersonal speech communication* is a term we have used to refer to what occurs when an individual interacts with another person, or with "a few" others. *Person-to-persons speech communication* is a term we are now using to designate what occurs when an individual speaks to a group of individuals.

It is difficult to draw an absolute line between interpersonal and person-to-persons speech communication. Six members of the editorial staff of a college newspaper may attend a meeting called by the dean to "discuss" with him the editorial policies of the newspaper. If the dean talks for ten or fifteen minutes at a stretch, describing his positions on various editorial policies, each of the students might say on reflection that they had been listening to a speech rather than engaging in any form of interpersonal communication. On the other hand, some college professors approach their classes in a very casual, informal way, encouraging considerable spontaneous interaction and constantly adapting themselves to the ideas and opinions expressed in class. Such professors, on reflection, might say that they are engaging in forms of interpersonal communication, even though a given class may number 50 or more students. The point is simply that a quantitative criterion is not sufficient in itself to distinguish between the levels of interpersonal and person-to-persons speech communication.

10.2. Some qualitative distinctions can be made between interpersonal and person-to-persons speech communication. These distinctions, taken collectively, can help us to understand better the unique nature of person-to-persons speech communication. They are not absolute distinctions, but are "more-or-less" kinds of differences between speech communication levels.

10.2.1. Person-to-persons speech communication is associated with greater specificity of intent on the part of the source. The source usually has a relatively well defined message to deliver, a particular goal to achieve, or some kind of reaction to elicit from his audience. Occasionally the source views his intent simply as the completion of a task, such as "I have to say a few words of welcome," "I have to give a speech presenting this award," or "The chairman is about to call on me to give the treasurer's report." Public-speaking situations are frequently categorized according to intents, such as to persuade, to inform, to entertain. At any rate, in person-to-persons speech communication the source has greater specificity of intent than is *usually* the case in interpersonal speech communication.

10.2.2. In person-to-persons speech communication there is greater centrality of control of communication processes. The responsibility for determining the communication content and pattern is usually assumed by, or delegated to, one individual or a very limited number of individuals. What is talked about and whether it is talked about in a monologic or dialogic manner are usually decided by the source. Occasionally, audience members intervene in ways which influence the content and pattern of the communication. Nevertheless, a distinction may still be made between interpersonal speech communication, wherein most or all participants play a more active role in determining communication content and pattern, and person-to-persons speech communication, which involves greater centrality of control.

10.2.3. Person-to-persons speech communication involves more clearly defined expectations on the part of receivers. Surveys, especially in public-speaking contexts, have shown that receivers consider sincerity, poise, and well chosen subject essential to effective public speaking[1]; student audience members preferred that speakers employ documented evidence to support arguments and contentions[2]; and receivers had certain expectations for sources to whom they would attribute high credibility, such as that the high-credibility source would be older, logical, reliable, similar to the receivers themselves, inspiring, informed, qualified, believable, proud, unselfish, stable, safe, concerned, refined, and would have foresight, a command of English, expert knowledge, and common sense.[3] These illustrative studies support the notion that receivers are likely to have well defined expectations for sources engaging in person-to-persons speech communication. Although the expectations are not always as formidable as those listed above, receivers involved in person-to-persons speech communication situations are likely to expect certain things from a source who presumes to command their attention and occupy their time. The more formal the speaking situation, the more formalized the expectations of receivers are likely to be.

10.2.4. Person-to-persons speech communication involves less differentiated perceptions of receivers by the source. In other words, the source is more likely to address his communication content to a "general other." In interpersonal speech communication the source is more likely to address his communication content to relatively well defined, specific others.

10.3. These factors combine to give person-to-persons speech communication a flavor very different from that of other speech

---

[1] W. K. Clark, "A Survey of Certain Audience Attitudes Toward Commonly Taught Standards of Public Speaking," *Speech Monographs*, 18 (March 1951), 62–69.

[2] Robert S. Cathcart, "Four Methods of Presenting Evidence," *Speech Monographs*, 22 (August 1955), 227–33.

[3] Jack L. Whitehead, "Factors of Source Credibility," *Quarterly Journal of Speech*, 54 (February 1968), 59–63.

communication levels. Indeed, consideration of these characteristics will yield a set of prescriptions which you should remember as you prepare to act as a source in a person-to-persons speech communication situation. The prescriptions become more applicable as the situation becomes more formal and receiver expectations become more formalized. In a public-speaking situation the following prescriptions might be considered the minimum essential considerations confronting a source. First, have a specific, well formulated purpose. Know what you want to say. Second, have in mind a general communication pattern you would like to follow. If you want to encourage receiver interventions for the purpose of asking questions, voicing differing opinions, or offering suggestions, tell the audience that you prefer this kind of communication pattern. If you prefer to proceed at your own rate through a prepared presentation, tell the audience that you prefer to wait until the end of the presentation for questions and discussion. Third, meet the minimum expectations of the audience: be prepared, know your topic, give evidence for your contentions, support your point with illustrations and examples that clarify complex information, and be sincere about your content and purpose. Even if your role as a source is unexpected and your speaking is an impromptu response to spontaneous developments, you should still attempt to approximate these prescriptions.

   Two relatively recent developments reinforce the importance of understanding the basic characteristics of person-to-persons speech communication. Both of these developments can be encapsulated by labels frequently applied to the present age: "information explosion" and "communication explosion." We are constantly bombarded with messages, appeals, compelling causes, and important information on topics and issues accompanied by exhortations demanding our attention and expecting our genuine interest. We are immersed in messages and media, and the competition for attention has had several results. One is an increased demand for, and use of, skilled and professional communicators to design and present messages. The second is that the professional communicators have developed an unprecedented bag of tricks, gimmicks, novel and imaginative devices, and strategies, sometimes explicit and sometimes very unobtrusive, to capture and hold our attention and interest. This is the climate in which you "speak." These are the messages with which your message competes. As we, acting as receivers, become less tolerant of attempts to persuade us and more despairing of our ability to accumulate and store information we are repeatedly told is vitally important to us, we must attempt to justify our acting as sources. If we fail to meet the minimum prescriptions outlined above, adding another voice to the cacophony that already exists seems somehow less justifiable.

10.4. Intent to Inform. Assume that you are planning a brief oral presentation to your class with the general purpose of informing, of helping the receivers acquire and retain information. Assume also that you have detailed, in your mind or on paper, your specific intent. You have outlined the major ideas you want the receivers to understand. You have identified the concepts which must be comprehended if the main ideas are to be appreciated. You have enumerated the details, the facts, the examples, and the illustrations which will help clarify the concepts and give them meaning for your receivers. Now let us raise and attempt to answer some general questions, and subsequently list some specific devices which might help you accomplish your goals.

First, how important is it that you select a topic that is inherently interesting to the audience? Petrie has summarized research on informative speaking and concludes that the audience's prior interest in a topic is not systematically related to receiver comprehension of content.[4] Although the research evidence is not conclusive, there is reason to believe that the arousal of interest during the speech influences the acquisition and retention of information. So it is probably not terribly important that you select a topic which has inherent appeal, but it *is* important that you devote some time early in your presentation to reasons why the receivers should be interested in what you are presenting. It is even more important that you select a topic in which *you* are genuinely interested. Your interest and enthusiasm, especially if such enthusiasm is channeled in productive directions, are likely to influence the receivers' interest and enthusiasm.

10.4.1. Given your interest in the topic, what general strategy is likely to result in greater comprehension and retention of information by the receivers? Petrie concludes that generalizations or major

[4]Charles R. Petrie, Jr., "Informative Speaking: A Summary and Bibliography of Related Research," *Speech Monographs*, 30 (June 1963), 79–91.

ideas, especially if they are well developed and supported in a number of ways, are better comprehended and retained than are details and specifics.[5] The general strategy implied is that you should not attempt to cover too much territory. Your presentation should be built around only a few well developed ideas which should be given several types of support. The supporting materials should be selected not so much for their inherent interest or appeal as for their value in developing and advancing the main ideas. A variety of very specific devices should be employed in the presentation of both main ideas and supporting materials. A brief list of some of the devices employed in informative speaking follows. You can add to this list and develop a mixture which will give your presentation an individual flavor.

1. *Repetition.* Professional users of the media have known for many years that repetition is an effective device, especially in getting listeners to recall products and brand names, even if the listeners dislike the repetition.[6] Yes, even if the receivers dislike repetitive messages or repetition of parts of messages, they are more likely to acquire and retain information when such information is repeated. Of course to increase the likelihood that they will acquire and retain the information, messages or message components need not be repeated to the point of alienating receivers. To reinforce the point, messages or message components that are repeated are more likely to be acquired and retained by receivers.

2. *Previewing.* Previewing means calling the audience's attention to a message component soon to be presented. Sometimes called "proactive emphasis," previewing consists of highlighting in advance message components you wish the audience to attend to and remember. It may be accomplished in the introductory comments, in which you outline briefly your major ideas and points, or through comments such as, "Now this next point is very important" or "Now I'm going to list the five cities which have the highest suicide rates in the United States. See if you can note any major similarities among these cities." Both previewing and repetition are implied in the traditional rhetorical admonition, "Tell them what you're going to tell them, tell them, and tell them what you told them."

[5] Petrie, p. 80.
[6] Hadley Cantril and G. W. Allport, *The Psychology of Radio* (New York: Harper & Row, Publishers, 1935).

3. *Variety and Emphasis.* Variety and emphasis incorporate many specific devices: pauses before key words or phrases; changes in vocal volume; changes in physical animation and gesturing. That variety and emphasis are effective devices might help explain the speech instructor's cautions against overreliance on notes during an oral presentation. Undue reliance on notes may tend to restrict physical movement and depress vocal variety. One way to attain greater variety and emphasis is through the effective use of the next-listed device.

4. *Visual Aids.* That visual aids increase the recall of information is another of Petrie's conclusions.[7] Indeed, it is sometimes possible to organize presentations or major parts of presentations around the use of visual aids. Properly prepared and displayed, visual aids are valuable in facilitating the acquisition and retention of information, as well as potentially useful in freeing the speaker from an overdependence on notes or manuscript. The speaker can frequently organize major parts of his presentation so that the visual aids serve also as his "notes" or reminders of what he is going to say and what topical order he will follow.

The adequate use of visual aids simply shows that you are following the basic principle elaborated in Chapter 6, that using several modalities is more likely to result in adequate processing of information on the part of receivers.

5. *Illustration and Example.* Speakers are frequently guilty of overreliance on their narrative to develop ideas, when an example may better illustrate the point they are trying to make. The use of illustration and example is frequently the most efficient and effective way to make a point. In a recent discussion of accuracy and understanding in interpersonal communication, Knapp was developing the point that even those individuals whom we would expect to maintain a high level of objectivity are frequently misled by their own subconscious subjectivity.[8] Knapp employed the following illustration:

[7] Petrie, p. 82.

[8] Mark L. Knapp, "Accuracy and Understanding," Chapter 2 in James C. McCroskey, Carl Larson, and Mark L. Knapp, *An Introduction to Interpersonal Communication* (Englewood Cliffs, N. J.: Prentice-Hall, Inc., 1971).

In connection with the qualitative characteristics of the brain, the early investigations of Bean (1906) have focused attention upon possible Negro–white differences. In a series of studies Bean arrived at the conclusion that the frontal area of the brain was less well-developed in the Negro than in the white, and the posterior area better developed. He believed that this difference paralleled the "known fact" that the Negro is inferior in the higher intellectual functions and superior in those concerned with rhythm and sense perception. Another important difference was in the depth of the convolutions of the cortex, those of the Negro being much shallower and more "childlike" than those of the white. There were also differences in the shape of the *corpus callosum*, which connects the two hemispheres of the cerebrum, and in the temporal lobe, but these were not regarded as having any direct psychological significance. It happened that these studies were carried out at Johns Hopkins University under the direction of Professor Mall, head of the Department of Anatomy. Mall (1909) was for some reason uncertain of Bean's results, and he repeated the whole study on the same collection of brains on which Bean had worked; he took the precaution, however, of comparing the brains without knowing in advance which were Negro and which were white. When he and his associates placed in one group those brains which had rich convolutions, and in another those with convolutions which were shallow, they found exactly the same proportions of Negro and white brains in the two groups. When further they measured the size of the frontal and posterior lobes in the two groups of brains, they found no difference in their relative extent. As a consequence, Mall came to the conclusion that Bean's findings had no basis in fact, and that it had not been demonstrated that Negro brains differed in any essential manner from those of whites.[9]

6. *Concrete Words.* Wherever possible you should describe the concepts and ideas you are developing in simple and concrete terms. This point is probably simple enough that a single example will reinforce it.

One of our friends is interested in concept formation in children. He is also interested in the impact of the environment, especially ghetto living, on the explanations children develop for things they observe. Our friend is fond of relating an incident involving a black family that had moved from a southern to a northern ghetto. During the first winter in the north one of the children in the family

[9] O. Klineberg, *Social Psychology* (New York: Holt, Rinehart and Winston, Inc., 1954).

encountered snow for the first time, and was so intrigued that he made a snowball and put it into his pocket to save. He hung up his coat inside and the next morning was dismayed to discover that the snowball had disappeared. He asked his mother what had happened to the snowball, and she jokingly replied, "What do you think happened to it?" The child replied, "I guess a rat must have ate it."

These six devices for helping receivers acquire and retain information are by no means all that are available to you. They are intended to be a "starter list." Keeping the audience in mind and planning your presentation to accomplish specific objectives will lead you to discover and possibly to invent additional devices consistent with a general intent to inform.

10.5. Intent to Persuade. Once again we ask you to recall the ideas we have developed concerning the interdependence of speech communication levels. What occurs at the person-to-persons level is reflected in the operation of each receiver's intrapersonal speech communication processes. The words you utter as a source comprise one set of communication content. The things the receivers tell themselves about you, your words, your demeanor, the situation, the allegiances that cross their minds as they listen to your words, and many other things comprise another set of communication content. The two communication contents are not necessarily similar or complementary. The extent to which they are similar is a function of your ability to trigger responses that are similar to your own. Presumably, the better you know a receiver, the more accurately you can anticipate his responses to various communication contents. Hence the speech teacher's admonition, especially in persuasive speaking, to analyze the audience.

Audience analysis is a broad and complex topic. The list of additional readings at the end of this chapter will lead you to more comprehensive treatments of this topic. Our present objective is to provide you with two basic perspectives from which to view audiences as you begin to plan a presentation with a general intent to persuade. These two perspectives are (1) taking into account the bases of beliefs, and (2) taking into account degrees of involvement.

10.6. Taking into Account the Bases of Beliefs. In Chapter 8 we developed the point that types of beliefs can be distinguished in terms of the bases underlying them. If you intend to influence how receivers talk with themselves about your message content, your appeal should be somehow related to the foundations on which the receivers' beliefs rest. It does you no good to appeal to authority when you are attempting to influence beliefs that are not based on authority. There is little point in introducing facts and statistics, no matter how impressive the array, when you are attempting to influence beliefs that are based on individual interpretations of experience. I cannot hope to employ facts and statistics to convince you that automobile drivers in the United States are overwhelmingly courteous and considerate if your experience has repeatedly told you otherwise. Consequently, one of the first steps in influencing an audience's beliefs about a certain content is the identification of the bases underlying such beliefs. Let us review briefly the types of beliefs identified in Chapter 8 and point out some tentative avenues to influencing these beliefs.

Type A. Primitive Beliefs, 100% Consensus, are rooted in a socially defined reality. They are true because we all believe that they are true. As a matter of fact, because these beliefs are based on social consensus, they are rarely attacked. On the few occasions when such beliefs are attacked we are likely to regard the attacker as bizarre, insane, or—more to the point—"out of touch with reality." What is required to influence such beliefs is supporting material demonstrating that a given belief is being increasingly questioned by a growing body of people, and that the people currently questioning the belief are some of the same individuals who previously comprised part of the social consensus underlying the belief. Such an approach is not likely to result in the conversion of the belief or the adoption of an opposite belief, but it may lessen the intensity with which the belief is held. With a "once only" presentation to an audience, a very small impact on Type *A* beliefs is all that can reasonably be expected.

Type B. Primitive Beliefs, 0% Consensus, grow from our peculiar interpretation of our experience with the world around us. These beliefs are not based on or maintained through social consensus. Many of our beliefs are of this type. Your evaluations of people, forms of social behavior and activity, and social institutions are frequently Type *B* beliefs. You have come to expect differences of opinion with respect to these beliefs, and you have acquired great skill, practice, and facility in defending them. From the sea of facts and statistics that surrounds us all it is not likely that I can select facts or statistics so overwhelmingly compelling as to influence your Type *B* beliefs. It is much more likely that these beliefs can be influenced through supporting material which relies on vivid imagery, dramatic illustration, material which triggers your recollection of past experiences, or material which calls for an empathic appreciation for the point of view being advanced. The material should be compelling in terms of the vicarious experiences it provides for the receivers, or else it should allow the receivers to relate a different set of their past experiences to the issue.

Type C. Authority Beliefs relate to our judgments about which specific sources or senders of messages can be relied on: what individuals, which groups, or even which large classes of individuals are likely to know and can be trusted to be truthful about what they know. Our authority beliefs are susceptible to change under any of three conditions: (1) if the authority cannot know what he claims to know; (2) if the authority does not really believe what he says he believes; and (3) if other authorities, equally or more well-regarded by the receiver, disagree with the authority in question. Many authority beliefs, though susceptible to change, are tenaciously held. Character assassination and smear tactics, although they may influence our evaluation of many others, are not likely to influence our confidence in those specific sources we have elevated to the rank of trusted and legitimized sources of information. Thus, attempts to influence authority beliefs should be undertaken only if you have substantial reasons for believing (1) that the authority, although he may sincerely believe in the validity of his position, is not in a position to know; (2) that there is good reason to suspect that the authority does not really hold the position attributed to him; or (3) that other highly regarded authorities disagree with him.

Type D. Derived Beliefs grow from our willingness to rely on certain sources of information for facts and descriptions of past and present realities, even though we may never have directly experienced the content of these beliefs. Hence, most of our derived beliefs are susceptible to change through exposure to facts, statistics, scientific and empirical evidence, and reports of direct observations.

So long as these materials are in some way documented or so long as our confidence in the factual nature of the material is somehow bolstered, we appear ready to accept such material. Note, however, that our acceptance of such material relates only to our derived beliefs, not necessarily to any of our other types of beliefs.

Type E. Inconsequential Beliefs, since they are matters of personal taste, are seldom the targets of persuasive attempts in person-to-persons speech communication situations, even though they may be the principal targets of mass media ads.

One way to view audience analysis, therefore, is to take into account the bases of the audience's beliefs. The minimum considerations growing from this perspective are implied in the following questions: (1) What specific beliefs am I ·attempting to influence? (2) What type or types of beliefs are these? (3) Why do these particular receivers hold the beliefs, and on what kinds of foundations do the beliefs rest? (4) In developing my points and ideas, what types of supporting material are likely to have impact on these specific receivers with respect to these specific beliefs?

10.7 Taking into Account Degrees of Involvement. Our beliefs about the world and the people in it are interspersed with a multitude of favorable or unfavorable predispositions toward people, objects, events, and circumstances.[10] Thus, on any given topic an individual may hold a variety of related attitudes.

10.7.1. If a relatively wide range of attitudes on a given topic are listed and arranged on a continuum from extremely positive to extremely negative, we could locate the attitudes of individuals and aggregates of individuals along that continuum. The perspective which emerges from such an approach is enlightening; we will adapt it from the work of Sherif, Sherif, and Nebergall.[11] To illustrate this perspective we must select an attitude object and identify an array of statements arranged along a continuum representing degrees of

[10] M. Fishbein, "A Consideration of Beliefs, Attitudes, and Their Relationship," in I. Steiner and M. Fishbein, eds., *Current Studies in Social Psychology* (New York: Holt, Rinehart and Winston, Inc., 1965).

[11] Carolyn Sherif, Muzafer Sherif, and Roger Nebergall, *Attitude and Attitude Change: The Social Judgment–Involvement Approach* (Philadelphia: W. B. Saunders Company, 1965).

positive and negative orientation toward that object. Any attitude object will do, but we have arbitrarily selected "pornography." The following statements, very subjectively created, represent our attempt to construct a range of attitudes with some crude distinctions between various points along the attitudinal continuum.

A. The federal and local governments should immediately intervene to control and censor all possession and display of pornographic material.

B. Much stricter laws should be passed regulating the possession and display of pornographic material.

C. Pornography is generally bad and its effects are detrimental.

D. Although I disapprove of pornography and consider some of its effects to be detrimental, I believe that the possession of pornographic material is largely a matter of individual conscience.

E. I neither approve nor disapprove of pornography. There are many important questions about it for which we have no answers, so no specific action or evaluation seems justified.

F. Pornography is not a bad thing; some of its effects may even be beneficial, or at least pleasant.

G. Interest in and possession of pornographic material is a natural, healthy, human phenomenon.

H. All current laws regulating the possession and display of pornographic material should be revoked.

I. Since social scientific evidence and the experience of several other nations demonstrate that pornography has a cathartic effect, the possession and display of pornographic material should be encouraged.

10.7.2. Assume, for the sake of the illustration, that each statement represents a different point along a continuum ranging from a negative evaluative orientation (A) to a positive evaluative orientation (I). Of course, individuals and groups differ in terms of their location along the continuum and the extent to which they are involved in or committed to their positions. To explicate the nature of this involvement or commitment, we introduce three concepts defined by Sherif, Sherif, and Nebergall[12] :

1. *Latitude of acceptance* is the position on an issue (or toward an object) that is most acceptable, plus other acceptable positions.

2. *Latitude of rejection* is the most objectionable position on the same issue, plus other objectionable positions.

[12] Sherif, Sherif, and Nebergall, p. 24.

3. *Latitude of noncommitment* encompasses those positions not categorized as either acceptable or objectionable in some degree.

To directly assess an audience's latitudes of acceptance, rejection, and noncommitment you would have to gather their responses to scales designed to measure their attitudes toward a given object. Most speech communication sources cannot or do not directly assess an audience's attitudes. Nevertheless, it is possible and appropriate to make a few reasoned guesses about the attitudinal profile of an audience you are attempting to influence. For example, assume that you are going to speak to an adult female service organization with a voluntary membership based on social affiliations. Your analysis of the audience along with the clues you have gathered from your contact with the program chairman and several other members of the organization lead you to expect the attitudinal profile represented in Figure 10.1.

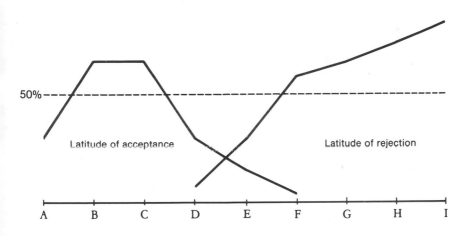

FIGURE 10.1   Hypothetical attitudinal profile.

10.7.3. More than half the receivers accept positions B and C as appropriate and legitimate attitudes to hold on pornography. Consequently, the latitude of acceptance for this group encompasses positions B and C. Similarly, more than half the receivers in this group regard positions F, G, H, and I as inappropriate, objectionable, or rejectable attitudes about pornography. Consequently, the latitude of rejection for this group encompasses positions F, G, H, and I. Most of the receivers in this group neither accept nor reject positions A, D, and E. These positions represent the group's latitude of noncommitment.

The degree of involvement for this group in the topic "pornography" is a function of the size of the latitude of rejection compared with the size of the latitude of acceptance, assuming relatively few positions on which the audience is noncommitted. So you are talking to a group that is relatively involved in the topic and committed to a rather narrow range of acceptable positions. How do you intend to influence this group's attitudes toward pornography? What general approach would you take in planning a message with such an intent? Give these questions some thought before you read on.

Most people attempt persuasion with an almost evangelical stance. They set out to oppose the audience's attitudes directly and they attempt to bring about a conversion of attitudes. We probably adopt such a confrontation stance because it is usually more self-gratifying and frequently more fun than any other. If a speech communication source is more interested in self-gratification than in affecting the receivers, then our present concern is irrelevant. On the other hand, if you are planning a presentation with the intent to persuade, you should keep in mind the following statement:

> A very considerable body of research shows that communication falling within the latitude of rejection is seen as discrepant by the subject, is appraised unfavorably as unfair, propagandistic, biased, and even false. In short, derogation of a communicator and his message—far from being an alternative to attitude change—occurs when the communication is within the latitude of rejection and appraised as greatly discrepant.[13]

Hence, we advise you not to attempt major conversions in the attitudes of involved or highly committed audiences. Such attempts at major conversion, based on direct confrontation of opposing points of view, are likely to result in the rejection of you as a speaker and the further entrenchment of audience attitudes.

10.7.4. With respect to the attitudinal profile shown in Figure 10.1, let us offer two speculations. First, some attitudinal movement might occur if the speaker argues against position A, that is, if he discusses the dangers involved in the widespread and strict control

[13] Sherif, Sherif, and Nebergall, p. 15.

and censorship of pornography and the potential and historical consequences of such control and censorship. The speaker is not directly assaulting the audience's attitudes. Nevertheless, he might attempt to demonstrate how adherence to position B might lead to the rigid controls implied by position A. Second, attitudinal movement might occur if the speaker supports positions D and E as appropriate and acceptable. The two speculations combined produce an approach that will not result in a reversal or conversion of attitudes. However, the change that results may still be much greater than that which would result from an attempt to support positions that are perceived by the audience as very discrepant with its latitude of acceptance.

10.7.5. Many speech communication sources have too narrow a view of what is meant by "attitude change." Many sources set out to change the location on an attitudinal continuum of the *most preferred* position of receivers. But attitude change may also be conceived of as a change in the *size* of the latitude of acceptance or the latitude of rejection. In other words, persuasive messages may also be planned and presented with an intent to elicit from an audience greater tolerance for, and appreciation of, a wider range of alternative points of view on a given topic. Such a conception of attitude change seems to us to imply persuasive attempts directed toward more desirable and reasonable goals. It implies that communicators, instead of saying, "You are wrong," would more frequently say, "There are other points of view that you may want to consider." A change in the size of the latitude of acceptance, or better yet, a change in the size of the latitude of rejection, represents attitude change as much as does a change in a receiver's or a group's most preferred position on an attitudinal continuum.

Many other important factors should be considered in planning and presenting communication content designed to inform or to persuade. Speech communication sources may have many other intents in planning and presenting communication content. The factors we have focused on in this chapter provide initial perspectives from which to view person-to-persons speech communication. The additional readings suggested for this chapter will help broaden and refine those initial perspectives.

SUMMARY

1. Person-to-persons speech communication differs from other levels of speech communication in that it is characterized by greater specificity of intent on the part of the source, more centralized control of the communication process, and more well defined expectations on the part of the receivers.

2. A speech communication source should take into account the basic expectations of the receivers.

3. When we act as sources, we are competing with a multitude of professional communicators for the attention and time of receivers.

4. A source who intends to inform should select a topic that interests him and build the presentation around a few main ideas.

5. Devices that may be employed to facilitate the acquisition and retention of information by receivers include repetition, previewing, variety and emphasis, visual aids, illustration, and concrete words.

6. A speech communication source who intends to persuade should analyze his receivers and attempt to anticipate their responses to his specific appeals.

7. Two basic factors to take into account when attempting to persuade are the bases underlying receiver beliefs and the degrees of receiver involvement and commitment.

8. Arguments and supporting materials should be related to the specific foundations on which receiver beliefs rest.

9. In planning a persuasive presentation, the source should attempt to estimate the receivers' latitudes of acceptance, rejection, and noncommitment.

10. Direct frontal assaults on receiver beliefs and attempts to support positions greatly discrepant from the attitudes of receivers are not likely to result in attitude change.

11. Changes in the sizes of the latitudes of acceptance and rejection may be regarded as attitude change.

EXERCISES

1. Plan and deliver to the class a presentation with the purpose of informing. Be sure that you have a specific purpose in mind. Before making the presentation, write down six questions you hope the receivers will be able to answer

adequately as a result of your presentation. At the conclusion of your presentation, read the six questions to the audience and ask them to write brief answers to each of the questions. Collect their answers, and review them on your own to assess the extent to which you accomplished your objectives.

2. Plan and deliver to the class a presentation with the purpose of persuading. Write down your specific purpose and the nature of the attitudinal change you are hoping to elicit. Give this statement to your instructor. At the conclusion of your presentation, if time allows, solicit feedback from the audience about those factors which, from the receivers' point of view, you did not adequately take into account. Also find out which factors in your presentation were most effective in accomplishing your specific objectives.

3. In small groups, identify and discuss some additional purposes, other than to inform or persuade, that frequently characterize person-to-persons speech communication. Identify and discuss some of the factors related to the effectiveness of presentations with these other purposes.

ADDITIONAL READINGS

Brooks, William D., *Speech Communication*, Part III, "Public Communication." Dubuque, Ia.: William C. Brown Company, Publishers, 1971.

Brown, Charles T., and Charles Van Riper, *Speech and Man*. Englewood Cliffs, N. J.: Prentice-Hall, Inc., 1966.

Clevenger, Theodore, Jr., *Audience Analysis*. Indianapolis: The Bobbs-Merrill Co., Inc., 1966.

Sherif, Carolyn, Muzafer Sherif, and Roger Nebergall, *Attitude and Attitude Change: The Social Judgment–Involvement Approach*. Philadelphia: W. B. Saunders Company, 1965.

Zelko, Harold P., and Frank E. X. Dance, *Business and Professional Speech Communication*. New York: Holt, Rinehart and Winston, Inc., 1965.

Chapter 11

EVALUATING

SPEECH

COMMUNICATION

11.1. In Alfred, Lord Tennyson's poem "The Charge of the Light Brigade" appear the lines,

Theirs not to make reply,
Theirs not to reason why,
Theirs but to do or die.

Yet what good is it for man to know what he knows, to be able to reason, if not precisely for the purpose of reasoning why? Man has reason so that he may try to fathom the forces that move himself and others, to search after the meaning of his own existence and that of his fellow creatures, to try constantly to improve his condition and the general human condition. To reason and to use the information acquired through reason for self-betterment and the betterment of others is one of man's challenges.

From birth we search after improvement, not to please the whims of others, but for our self-fulfillment, comfort, pleasure, and self-respect. The infant laboriously crawls, eventually pulls himself up to his feet, falls, and rises and falls again. Only after innumerable attempts does he finally succeed in walking. The child walks not to please others, but to please himself. Of course, in the process of walking to please himself he also pleases his watching parents. Eventually he uses his ability to walk to please others by running errands, playing ball, and so on. He learns to walk through trial and error. The average child learns to walk whether or not someone tries to assist him. Human beings share an overpowering desire to do whatever they think they can do—walk, sing, play the piano, run bases, ride horses, build machines, read manuscripts, write books, or make trips into outer space.

11.2. Generally there is not one right way to engage in human speech communication. The most desirable speech communication, in our eyes, is that which enables an individual to actualize his potentialities more fully so that through self-improvement he can improve the human condition.

The improvement of the human condition by our personal efforts to encourage the development of others and of all mankind seems a worthwhile goal for each of us. A hopeless goal? Not so! Often it takes just a little motion, a short word, a quick glance, to ease another's burdens and by so doing to multiply our personal value and potency.

Evaluation almost always seems to be threatening because it causes us to expose ourselves, to be vulnerable to the judgment and criticism of others. Yet if we are bent on acquiring a skill such as playing the guitar or pleasing someone we love, we seek as much help as possible in learning to do the thing well.

When our efforts are characterized by a strong desire to succeed, we seem better able to transform the threatening aspects of evaluation into helpful criticisms. Of course, even so there is a limit beyond which the level of threat may become so high as to inhibit almost any activity. When you are engaged in a competitive sport and someone is hypercritical of you, you sometimes become so confused and threatened that you severely reduce your spontaneous participation in the game. However, generally those who offer evaluation of your speech communication behavior are working for you rather than against you, and seldom if ever will the level of criticism reach such threatening heights.

11.3. It is extremely difficult to perceive accurately how we appear to others. The older we grow, the harder it becomes to discover our image in the eyes of others. The reason is simple: in our society, age is usually accompanied by an increase in power within the societal structure. The more powerful you are, the less likely it is that responding others will let you know accurately and adequately how they feel about you. Compounding the difficulty of assessing how we appear to others and how our behaviors are viewed by others is the level of confidence we have in our self-image. If we think we are good or have an exalted opinion of ourselves, then it becomes difficult either to perceive or to accept others' negative evaluations of us. All of us know someone who we feel has a self-image that is higher than his general behavior pattern seems to warrant. We are also aware that the projection of one's high self-esteem is often, in actuality, a façade erected to hide a self-opinion which is actually lower than his potentialities or actualities warrant. The plea here is for each of us to try to assess himself as adequately and accurately as possible so that he can establish a base line from which to measure his successful or unsuccessful self-actualization. We need to recognize that it is easier to *distort* others' evaluations of ourselves than it is to acquire accurate evaluations of ourselves from others. To improve ourselves, to actualize as many of our potentialities as possible, we must have as accurate a self-image as we can acquire. But to acquire an accurate and adequate self-image, we must allow others to feel that they can help us in our effort to formulate a total congruent self-image.

We do not mean to suggest that all of an individual's behavior should be shaped by how others feel about him. What we are saying is that the individual, in deciding how successful or unsuccessful he is in terms of his goals and motivations, needs to have as accurate an understanding as possible of the effect of his behavior on responding others.

11.4. Successful evaluation should suggest ways of achieving greater behavioral success through the processes of addition to, deletion from, or substitution within our speech communication repertoire. Evaluation which becomes carping or capricious fault-finding or reflects the critic's personal dislike of the speaker is poor evaluation, not to be sought after or encouraged in ourselves or in others. From previous chapters we are aware that words reflect thoughts; therefore, when we evaluate the words of another or of ourselves, we are simultaneously evaluating thoughts. To pass judgment on the thinking of another person is a serious matter. It should be done as helpfully and as delicately as possible. A famous Englishman, Isaac D'Israeli, spoke of a friend who was able to ". . . wreathe the rod of criticism with roses." St. Paul exhorts us "to do the truth in charity." The goal of evaluation of speech communication is the improvement of self and eventually of others. The improvement of self is a delicate operation which calls for sensitivity and openness on the part of both the evaluator and the person being evaluated. The spoken word is man's chief instrument of individual and social progress, of the quest after truth and the search for justice. As such, we should respect it and do our best to elevate its use by ourselves and by others.

11.5. Through evaluation we seek behavioral self-improvement. The single best means of behavioral self-improvement is the conscious, planned alteration of future behavior based on the intelligent and informed appraisal of past and current behavior. The foregoing statement is based on the concept of feedback, which we borrow from the field of cybernetics. If we really want to improve our speech communication behavior, it is not enough to depend on chance or sporadic effort. We have to assess where we are, establish a base line, plot ways of moving ourselves beyond that base line, and then engage in the actual planned behaviors which result in improved speech communication. After having made these adjustments, we need once again to assess the success or failure of our new behavior.

11.5.1. How do we go about the process of assessment? Through feedback, a device for self-assessment. Internal feedback is the feedback we provide for ourselves, a form of intrapersonal speech communication. Positive internal feedback occurs when our appraisal of our current speech communication behavior indicates success and tells us that we should continue doing what we have been doing in the past. Negative internal feedback occurs when our assessment of our current speech communication behavior indicates that we are failing, and we decide to stop the kinds of behaviors we have engaged in in the past. There is also external feedback, provided through others' appraisal of us. External feedback can also be either positive, telling us that our speech communication is successful and that we can engage in more of the same behavior, or negative, suggesting that our speech communication behavior has been less successful than we desire and that we should alter our future behavior with the goal of making it more successful.

11.5.2. Exactly what are we appraising? On what do we seek feedback? Obviously, on our performance, our speech communication behavior. It is impossible to adequately appraise someone's intent. Intent and motivation can be inferred only from the behaviors that we ourselves manifest or that we observe in others. Therefore, the thing that we appraise is overt speech communication behavior. Although some aspects of appraisal are simple, they are still important. For instance, volume: is the speaker speaking too loudly so that he is intimidating, or too softly so that he is not heard; pace: is he speaking too fast or too slow; word selection: are his words suited to the level of comprehension of his audience and to the level of complexity of the subject matter; timing: does the length of his speech communication fall within the bounds of appropriateness as dictated by the time available, the number of others who have a right to be heard, the complexity of the subject matter, the level of comprehension of the listeners, and the occasion. There is nothing more annoying than the interminable speaker who makes a point and then insists on making it over and over until the listener is no longer interested in the point, but just in his hope that the speaker will stop talking. In formal speaking it is harder to give a short speech than a long one. The good and prudent speaker is challenged to make continuing selections from the wealth of material on his topic to keep his speech communication within appropriate time limits. One of the major differences between artful speech communication and rambling is exactly this process of selectivity. Another aspect of speech communication behavior that we can assess is the appropriateness of the mode and the channel chosen by the sender. Although we have been primarily concerned with speech communication and the centrality of the spoken word, there are times when the background noise is so great that vocal speech communication is inappropriate. Then we would choose a mode that uses the visual analyzer or the tactile analyzer, and the channel might be light rather than sound. On most occasions, however, we engage in vocal speech communication and we can assess our appropriate use of mode and channel in terms of whether we use audio-visual aids and whether those audio-visual aids help us achieve our specific purpose.

Using present experimental research information, we could argue about exactly what effect a speaker's organization has on the listeners' comprehension and reaction to any given speech communication event. Even so, the generalized experience of speech communicators suggests that organization in planning a speech communication event will help the speech communicator make selections of material. In a planned speech communication experience on the third level of person-to-persons, the organization often takes the form of a speech outline. Outlining for the sake of outlining is busy work; outlining for the sake of successful speech communication provides invaluable assistance to the speech communicator, both in planning his speech and in appraising its effect.

11.6. We have suggested appraisal of speech communication behavior through feedback. What are the criteria in terms of which we can make an adequate and accurate appraisal? Speech communication may be appraised in terms of its intent, its goals, its congruity, and its observable success.

Intent. What was our intention in a particular speech communication event? Did we, in fact, have a conscious intent, or was that communication event accidental? Is there any indication that we achieved our intent? Our intent guides us in the selection of our goals.

Goals. Goals are established on the basis of our intent, if our intent is conscious. Goals differ from intent in being organized in terms of the behaviors of others rather than in terms of our own needs, feelings, or desires. Whereas our intent may be to win the support of those with whom we are communicating, our goals for the specific event might be to persuade the listeners to contribute ten cents each, immediately, to the fund drive. Success in achieving our goal or goals often indicates that we have also been successful in achieving our intent; however, we should remember that reasons which cause us to achieve our goal may have nothing to do with our intent. Perhaps the pressure of seeing others give money causes some people to contribute without having a corresponding inner conviction to support the speaker's cause. In such a case the goal is being reached even though the speaker's intent is not satisfied. When formally stated on an outline, goals are sometimes known as specific purposes. A specific purpose should always be stated in terms of observable outcomes, so that the success or failure of the speech communication can be appraised more easily. For example, if our goal is to persuade the members of the audience, on this occasion, to give a minimum of five cents to the campaign fund, the success or failure of the goal can easily be evaluated by dividing a head count into the total sum collected. Again, we should not depend completely on such an empirical measure since some members of the audience who are in sympathy with our intent and our goal may not have any money with them. The point of the accurately phrased specific purpose is to provide the speaker with a guide to the selection of his content—include in the speech that which will help you achieve your specific purpose, no more and no less—as well as with a means of measuring his speech communication success or failure.

11.6.1. The goals of oneself and others often differ. The goals of the listeners should also be considered when appraising speech communication. What did the listener have in mind when he decided to participate in the speech communication event? Listener expectations are shaped by listener motivations, intent, and goals as well as by the occasion. What does the listener need to learn, want to hear, desire to do? The ethical speech communicator honestly assesses his listeners' expectations with the desire to achieve as much satisfaction for the listener as for himself and with the firm resolve to avoid manipulating his listeners to achieve speaker intent at the expense of listener intent and well-being.

Congruity means the compatibility among intent, goals, and speech communication behavior. Do our goals, in terms of what we expect from our listeners, manifest our intent or hide it? Are we manipulating our listeners, or are we trying to communicate openly and honestly with them? Have we tried to be honest with ourselves in seeking out our deepest intents?

Is the level on which we are communicating appropriate to the goals of the communication? For example, are we trying to achieve level three behavioral changes (person-to-persons) by using level two (interpersonal) speech communication, when in the interests of efficiency and openness level three speech communication would be more congruous?

Does our speech communication exhibit role congruity? Are we trying to suggest to our listener that we are acting out of friendship when we are actually acting out of self-interest? Do we use the visible signs of friendship (a smile) and the auditory signs of authority (a commanding voice, word selection allowing little choice on the part of the listener)? Do we make things difficult for the listener by confusing him with two or more roles (I am parent *and* friend when I am talking to you, or teacher, employer, and pal)?

Believing that speech communication is ethically meant to reveal rather than to obscure truth, does our speech communication help others to see us or does it only succeed in hiding us? The ancient concept of ethos may also be viewed within role congruity. Does our experience belie our age, or vice versa? Perhaps we look too young (age role) for the kind of information we are communicating (experience role)—thus creating some role incongruity within the listeners. Our job then is to reduce this role incongruity by revealing to our listeners that we are older than we look or that we have had unusual experiences for someone our age. Does our behavior usually appear manipulative while our speech communication calls for openness? Such incongruity often reduces possible goal achievement. As far as possible, speech communication behavior and other performance behavior should be congruous.

Observable Success. This simply means, did we achieve our speech communication goals? If so, why? If not, why not? How can we make our future speech communication behavior more successful?

11.7. Giving and Receiving Appraisal. When you are asked to appraise the speech communication of others, it is most helpful to move from the general to the specific. Comments about the overall success or failure of the speech, such as "I liked it" or "I didn't like it," "It was good" or "It was bad," are not very helpful. To improve our speech communication behavior, most of us need specific information, such as "The examples you gave were really helpful," "You went at just the right speed," "I could hear you clearly without feeling that you were yelling at me," "Next time try to slow down a bit," "I missed the connection between the point you were trying to make and the evidence you gave in its support. Next time I think you'd better work out the argument more closely if you really want to convince me." Appraisals should be characterized by sincerity and warmth. Our task when giving an appraisal is not to make the speaker feel bad but to help him achieve self-actualization as an effective speech communicator. Appraisals should be as brief and specific as possible.

When receiving appraisal we should remember that the evaluator is seeking to help us, and we should listen for points we can readily work into our speech communication behavioral repertoire. If we fail to understand something that the evaluator says, we should ask immediately for clarification and continue our questioning until we understand perfectly.

We should be generous in our acceptance of evaluations, whether they are negative or positive. Obviously, there is no point in arguing with an evaluation; you cannot tell someone that he did not feel as he said he did. All you can do is try to understand the evaluation in terms of your intent, your goals, and the principle of congruity in speech communication. Many speakers have difficulty in accepting positive evaluation. When praised for your speech communication, you also should generously acknowledge the compliment.

SUMMARY

1. The most desirable speech communication is that which enables an individual to actualize his potentialities more fully so that he can through self-improvement improve the human condition.

2. When we really want to succeed we are able to make good use of evaluation and appraisal.

3. The more powerful you are, the harder it is to determine accurately and adequately how you and your behaviors are viewed by responding others.

4. Good evaluation should help us achieve greater speech communication success through the process of addition, deletion, or substitution.

5. The single best means of behavioral self-improvement is the conscious, planned alteration of future behavior based on intelligent and informed appraisal of past and current behavior.

6. Feedback can be internal and/or external, positive and/or negative.

7. We appraise overt speech communication behavior (volume, pace, word selection, timing, organization) in terms of intent, goals, congruity, and observable success.

8. Ethical speech communication is meant to reveal rather than to obscure truth.

9. Appraisals should be characterized by briefness, specificity, warmth, sincerity, and helpfulness.

10. Appraisals should be received openly with the purpose of self-improvement. Negative appraisals should be understood but not argued with, and positive appraisals should be understood and appreciated.

EXERCISES

Since the student has been engaged in giving and receiving appraisals throughout the course, it seems unnecessary to include additional exercises in speech communication evaluation.

ADDITIONAL READINGS

Cathcart, Robert S., *Post Communication, Criticism and Evaluation*. Indianapolis: The Bobbs—Merrill Co., Inc., 1966.

Larrabee, Harold A., *Reliable Knowledge*. Boston: Houghton Mifflin Company, 1945.

Chapter 12

SYNTHESIS

12.1. Only hopeless pedants live daily lives characterized by textbook specificity. Anyone who goes through each day labeling all of the speech communication levels, functions, modes, and roles he encounters is well on the way to either confinement or social isolation. We simply do not live that way. When all of the detail and structure of scholarship is finally filtered through life experience, what we hope to find is a residue of practicality— knowledge that really helps us to live happier and more fruitful lives.

The synthesizing core of all that we have discussed in this book is simply (and unbelievably complicated) the individual acting out his life. Speech communication is act, activity, process, and in an individual's speech communication activity we see that individual's use and integration of levels, functions, and modes made manifest.

In role enactment we find the living synthesis of all elements of speech communication. If the theory presented in this textbook has any validity or usefulness, then that applicability must be found in the way we live our daily lives. What is more, the theory should help us predict speech communication behaviors, and we should be able to use it to improve speech communication behaviors. There simply is no true theory that is wrong in practice. If the theory has been correctly applied and fails in practice, then the theory is wrong in essence, not in application.

12.2. If we start at birth, the very outset of social life, and watch the infant begin to develop a self-concept, we can focus on that development from the point of view of level (level one? levels one and two? or levels two and three?), from the point of view of function (function one?), or in terms of the modes being used. However, such fractionalizing scrutiny must be synthesized into role, into the shaping of the infant's self-concept (which is, of course, deeply affected by the responding others in the infant's environment).

Throughout life a person moves through varying roles, displaying in each a slightly different constellation of speech communication levels, functions, and modes. When the constellation exhibits what we consider an appropriate or acceptable balance, we tend to accept the individual's speech communication behaviors as falling within the range called average or normal. When the constellation seems warped or incongruent, we often question, either covertly or overtly, the appropriateness of that person's speech communication behavior.

Speech communication assists the human being in the processes of self-actualization and of linking with his environment. The functional progression of speech communication is necessary for individual maturation throughout life. Mature speech communication is that which contributes most to the individual's self-actualization and successful linking with his environment. The regulation of the behavior of self and of others is, then, the result of conscious intent; it is almost always directed to the fulfillment of either self-actualization or the successful linking of the individual with his environment.

12.3. Speech communication is also intimately bound to mental health. The dynamic interrelationship of the three levels means that any marked decrement on one level has an effect on the other two levels. If a person is unable to establish congruence on the first level of speech communication between his feelings and his self-perception, this lack of congruence will almost inevitably appear on the second and third levels as well. Conversely, a relatively normal and stable individual may, through the efforts of manipulative others, be forced to participate in such warped second or third level speech communication events that his previously established normal patterns of first level speech communication become distorted. Brainwashing, seduction, and coercive persuasion are examples of such a course of action. Congruent speech communication on all three levels contributes to an individual's mental health.

12.4. Varying geometric models have been suggested to represent the speech communication process. The process is neither linear nor circular. Obviously, one's future speech communication is affected by one's past and present speech communication—there is some feedback, not just a simple progression. Just as obviously, our speech communication never concludes exactly where it began—there is some forward movement. The geometric model which may be most helpful is the helix, similar to the thread of a screw, or an extended "slinky" toy held upright. When viewed as helical, one's speech communication at one and the same time moves forward and yet gracefully curves back on itself in progressive motion. The intertwining of two or more helices, as in interpersonal or person-to-persons speech communication, is reminiscent of the double helix of genetic structure and testifies to the fantastic and fascinating complexity of human speech communication. An individual's speech communication is never truly discontinuous; there is always the connecting thread of individual being. This filament of sameness mirrors the dynamic interrelationship of levels, functions, and modes *in* role.

The synthesis is *you*; it is never a final synthesis, but rather always an emerging one. Because speech communication is uniquely human and uniquely humanizing, each of us must bend his interest and efforts toward an ever richer understanding of our unique gift, with the goal of self-actualization and social betterment.

SUMMARY

1. In role enactment we find the living synthesis of all elements of speech communication.

2. Mature speech communication is that which contributes most to the individual's self-actualization and successful linking with his environment throughout his life.

3. Congruent speech communication contributes to individual and societal mental health.

4. The helix may be the most helpful geometric model for considering speech communication.

5. The thread of individual being connects all of a person's speech communication and mirrors the dynamic interrelationship of levels, functions, and modes *in* role.

6. The synthesis of speech communication functions, levels, modes, and roles is *you*; it is never a final synthesis, but always an emerging one.

EXERCISES

1. We have suggested that we find the living synthesis of all of the elements of speech communication in individual role enactment. Using a deductive process, view a living celebrity (intellectual, political, social, performing arts, athletics, or the like) as the exemplification of a particular role. Describe the role and then analyze it in terms of how it is made up by specific levels, functions, and modes.

2. Using an inductive process, decide on a particular overall role which you would like to create (much as a playwright might decide on what specific type of character he wishes to portray) and then construct that role, using the levels, functions, and modes in differing relationships to produce a particular constellation. (For example, a warm personality might concentrate on level one, function one, and a dominance of very personal modes such as touch in structuring his speech communication.)

3. Try to create a visual representation of the interrelationships among levels, functions, modes, and roles. The final product could be anything from a chart or table to a collage, a montage, or a sculpture.

ADDITIONAL READINGS

Dance, Frank E. X., "A Helical Model of Communication," pp. 103–7 in *Foundations of Communication Theory*, eds. Kenneth K. Sereno and C. David Mortensen. New York: Harper and Row, Publishers, 1970.

Rogers, Carl R., *On Becoming a Person*. Boston, Mass.: Houghton Mifflin Company, 1961.

Wiener, N., *The Human Use of Human Beings: Cybernetics and Society*. 2nd rev. ed. Garden City, N. Y.: Doubleday & Company, Inc., 1954.

INDEX

A

Abrahams, D. 144
acceptance, latitude of 166
actualization (*see* self-actualization)
Adler, Mortimer J. 45–46
agent (*see* stimulus)
Allport, G. W. 159
analyzers (*see* primary analyzers)
Andrew, Richard J. 105
animal communication:
  compared to human communication
    40–47
  use of sign in 10, 11, 40–47
anthroposemiotic communicative
    behaviors 40, 42–43
Aquinas, Saint Thomas 47
Ardrey, Robert 41, 42
Argyle, Michael 110
Aristotle 13
Arnheim, Rudolf 27, 126
Aronson, V. 144
articulated sound (*see* sound,
    articulated)
attitudes 165
attitudinal profile 167
audio-visual aids 103
auditory modality, as primary analyzer
    95–98
Auer, J. Jeffrey 9, 10
authority beliefs 134, 164

B

babbling 76
Baker, Sidney J. 23

Baker model of communication 23–25
Baldridge, B. 146
Barker, Larry L. 11, 19, 61, 123, 124,
    127
Barnlund, Dean C. 8, 106, 122, 141,
    153
Bateson, Gregory 61, 72
Beavin, Janet 141
behavior, regulation of:
  as function of speech communication
    85–89
  and role 110–111
Beisecker, Thomas D. 139
beliefs:
  authority beliefs 134, 164
  in person-to-persons speech
    communication 162–165
  primitive beliefs 132–133, 163–164
Bellugi, Ursula 42
Bennis, Warren G. 140
Berelson, Bernard 3, 7
Berger, Joseph 19
Berlo, David K. 21, 22
Berlo model of communication 21–22
Berlew, David E. 140
Bernstein, Basil 79
Berry, Mildred Freburg 96, 98
Biddle, Bruce J. 122
Birdwhistell, Ray 101
Bloom, Benjamin S. 127
Borden, George A. 61, 137
Brewer, M. B. 149
Brewer, R. E. 146, 149
Brislin, R. W. 144
broadcast transmission 34